C0-APL-604

SUNNYVALE

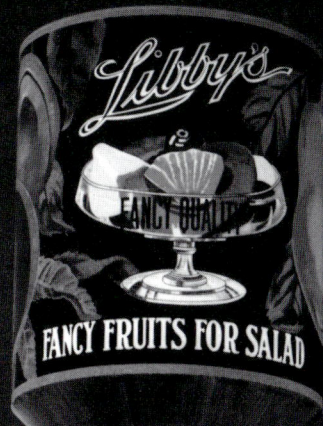

FROM THE CITY OF DESTINY TO THE HEART OF SILICON VALLEY

by Mary Jo Ignoffo

WITH A FOREWORD
BY MIKE MALONE

CALIFORNIA
HISTORY CENTER
& FOUNDATION
CUPERTINO,
CALIFORNIA

LOCAL HISTORY
STUDIES VOLUME 35

Sponsored by major donations from the following individuals and organizations: City of Sunnyvale, Bank America Foundation, Helen Kennedy Cahill, Rose Olson Memorial Fund, Dolly Stowell, and Sourisseau Academy/ San Jose State University.

Managing editor, N. Kathleen Peregrin

Copyright © by California History Center Foundation, 1994. All rights reserved, including the right of reproduction in any form.
Published by the California History Center & Foundation, De Anza College, 21250 Stevens Creek Blvd., Cupertino, California 95014.

10 9 8 7 6 5 4 3 2 1

First Edition

Library of Congress Cataloging-in-Publication Data

Ignoffo, Mary Jo, 1955-
       Sunnyvale from the city of destiny to the heart of Silicon Valley/by Mary Jo Ignoffo.
              p. cm. — (Local history studies; v. 35)
              Includes bibliographical references and index.
              ISBN 0-935089-17-9
              1. Sunnyvale (Calif.) — History. I. Title. II. Series.
F869.S86I36 1994
979.4'73--dc20

94-9363
CIP

COVER PHOTO:
The electric "Sunnyvale" sign marking the "highway entrance" at what today is El Camino Real and Murphy Avenue. It was installed by Hendy Iron Works in 1921 and paid for by contributors from the community. Courtesy Sunnyvale Historical Society & Museum Association.

TITLE PAGE PHOTO:
Former Libby Cannery water tower disguised as a fruit cocktail can, refurbished by artist Anita Kaplan. Courtesy City of Sunnyvale.

BACK COVER PHOTO:
"Sunnyvale" electric sign is dismantled circa 1942. Note the adjacent sign pointing to the Army Air Station. Moffett Field was under the jurisdiction of the Army from 1935 until 1942. Courtesy Sunnyvale Historical Society & Museum Association.

CONTENTS

ACKNOWLEDGEMENTS

<u>Sunnyvale From the City of Destiny to the Heart of Silicon Valley</u> began as a master's thesis completed at San Jose State University in 1991. Many people have encouraged and contributed to this work and deserve heartfelt thanks. Although impossible to name them all, the following deserve special recognition.

Thesis director N. Grey Osterud spent many hours discussing, reading, critiquing and encouraging which helped to develop the themes found in this community history. Dan Cornford's analysis helped to set the story of Sunnyvale in the context of California's history and expand the bibliography. Both went well beyond the call of duty and office hours to be available. Billie Jensen also of SJSU, served as another thesis reader offering useful suggestions.

The California History Center Foundation facilitated an internship to update the story of Sunnyvale. Former Director Jim Williams encouraged the work, gave insightful criticism, and previewed the final text. Present Director Kathleen Peregrin personally supported the project and coordinated the actual production of the book. She was attentive and available throughout the process. Librarian Lisa Christiansen was very generous with her time and the CHC collection, often helping to track down obscure or rare sources and photographs. Members of the Board of Trustees of the CHCF offered encouragement and help especially Yvonne Jacobson and Ward Winslow.

This book would not have been possible were it not for the enthusiastic support of the Sunnyvale Historical Society & Museum Association, especially President Mignon Trice and museum curators Howard and Chiyo Winters. They offered personal assistance with photographs and the museum archive collection and provided information about longtime Sunnyvale families. Together with the historical society, Sunnyvale's Heritage Preservation Commission endorsed this project. Many board members and commissioners offered personal support, especially Joe Gutierrez, Bev Walz, and Glen Weaver.

Sunnyvale Public Library has a treasure trove of Sunnyvale memorabilia, clippings, scrapbooks and government documents available to the public. The staff there was very helpful in providing a great research source, especially Shirley Clements, Mary Walsh Winklebleck and Bev Walz.

Most of the photographs appearing here are from the historical society and the California History Center. Others also lent photos including Linda Crabill (City of Sunnyvale), Julia O'Keefe (Santa Clara University Archives), Ed Fassett, S.J., Edwina Brackenbury, and Ann Zarko. Their images help to tell this story.

Funding was provided by a variety of individuals and community and business groups, and each was crucial to the production of this book. Special recognition for fundraising belongs to Yvonne Jacobson, Miriam Stelling, Mignon Trice, Margaret Wozniak, Pete Keim, and Janet Brynjolfsson.

Thanks are due to those who previewed the text and offered their comments. They are Ann Hines, Caroline Ryan, Howard Winters, Mike Malone, Yvonne Jacobson, Jim

Williams, Kathi Peregrin and Lisa Christiansen. Others agreed to be interviewed and they are Harriet Willson, Kay Peterson, Ed Fassett, S.J., Larry Stone, Dorothy Miller, Caroline Ryan and Ann Hines. Those who spoke to me in a less formal setting included Mary Miholovich, Jo Givich Handel, Mignon Trice and Suzanne Mulcahy. I am grateful to John Ignoffo, Jr. for help with the computer and Laura Miller for help with property deeds.

Many personal friends and family members offered moral support throughout the evolution of this book. My husband, Pat Ignoffo and my parents Helen and Sandy Hull to whom this book is dedicated, have been a continual source of encouragement. My brothers and sisters (Sandy, Mike, Laura, Debbie and Miriam) and friends have often asked about the progress of this project. I appreciate the concern and interest especially from Joan, Gerri, Dan, Bob, Karen, Ed, Sharon, Susan & Bob and Grey Osterud who became a good friend.

To those of you who contributed to this book in so many ways, I thank you.

For
HELEN AND SANDY HULL
who gave me my history
and for
my friend, partner and husband
PAT IGNOFFO
and our little boy
JOEY.

FOREWORD

Here's why you need to read this book. If you live in Sunnyvale, even if you've only been a resident for a week, you need to read this book because this is your history. The political battles and business neighborhood skirmishes that take place every day in this city are the result of forces decades, even centuries, old. After reading <u>Sunnyvale From the City of Destiny to the Heart of Silicon Valley</u>, you'll realize that many of the characteristics of this city that seem so inexplicable suddenly become understandable, the product of some pivotal decision made in a forgotten — until now — past.

To read the story of Sunnyvale is to realize that no matter what new challenge faces us, it can be overcome by smart, committed people. For example, Moffett Naval Air Station, which was such a critical influence in the creation of this city, and of the rest of Santa Clara Valley, was built here as the result largely of the efforts of a single, dedicated woman. This book is filled with such vital people, and they are no different from ourselves.

Finally, if you live in Sunnyvale, you need to read this book to become angry: at exploitative growers and racist laws and a mindless belief in progress that led to the destruction of some of our most important and beautiful historic buildings. It is to Mary Jo Ignoffo's credit that she flinches from none of these painful truths . . . and it is a call to each of us never to let such tragedies happen again.

If, on the other hand, you live outside Sunnyvale, let me tell you a story.

On the west side of Sunnyvale, in the midst of several housing developments and beside a freeway, there is a nondescript intersection of two roads, Bernardo and Fremont avenues. It is so featureless that even if you had to sit there for a red light you would never remember it. Yet, it can be argued with near certainty, that on some late afternoon in the the late '60s or early '70s, three individuals were at or near that intersection at the same time: Young Steve Wozniak, riding his bicycle home from swim practice at the Cherry Chase swim club; Ted Hoff, who lived just a couple doors down from the corner; and Hoff's boss, Dr. Robert Noyce, driving home to Los Gatos from his newly founded company, Intel, based in Santa Clara.

Just three anonymous people, at an anonymous intersection in a city that has often been characterized as the very archetype of anonymous suburbia. And yet. . .

The three men at that chance encounter would be remembered as the creators of the integrated circuit, the microprocessor and the personal computer, perhaps the three most important inventions of the 20th century. A few years later, at a bar on the other side of town, Nolan Bushnell would install a new kind of electronic pinball game with which he was experimenting. He called it Pong. When, after just a few hours, the bar's owner called to complain that the machine had broken down, Bushnell went rushing down to discover the real problem was that the coin tray was overstuffed with quarters. Thus, the video game industry began in Sunnyvale, too — as did the design of the Space

Shuttle and many U.S. military aircraft and ballistic missiles.

So much for anonymous. The reality is that Sunnyvale has been the most important American city in the second half of this century. That is a bold statement. But it is true. Think about that intersection: You would have to go back to Paris in the 1920s or London in the 1890s or New York in the 1870s to find such a juxtaposition of famous figures.

But Sunnyvale is important for another reason as well. No other community has seen such change in such a short time. Sunnyvale is a microcosm of all American cities in the postwar era. Introverted and parochial, yet industrious and friendly, Sunnyvale suddenly found itself swept up in one revolution after another — high technology, the Pacific Rim, the rise of suburbia, the Baby Boom, the global marketplace — and fought to stay atop each wave. Remarkably, it succeeded. As Mary Jo Ignoffo so well describes it, at the end of the Second World War, Sunnyvale was a sleepy little farmtown whose self-applied moniker — The City of Destiny — sounded like (and was) a real estate agent's hustle. By 1993, when the president and vice-president of the United States flew to Sunnyvale to declare it the best run city in America and a model for governments everywhere, the nickname suddenly rang true.

Just how Sunnyvale not only survived, but triumphed, is told here for the first time. The story should be read by every city manager, every mayor and city council member, every chamber of commerce official hustling new industries and every no-growth activist in the country. In these pages you will find your counterpart. You can triumph in their victories, weep at their losses, and most of all, learn from their mistakes. It would be marvelous achievement if, in the end, Sunnyvale's greatest contribution to American culture was as an exemplar of what to do right — and what not to do wrong — in building a modern city.

I grew up in Sunnyvale. I bought my first Boy Scout uniform at Kirkish's and went to movies at the theater on Murphy Street. I played tennis at Fairbrae and opened my first bank account in Westmoor Village. I went to Fremont High School with the grandchildren of orchardists and the children of high-tech tycoons.

Along the way I met many of the men and women who appear in these pages. Among the thousands, three experiences in particular stand out.

The first took place on a cool November morning in 1978. I was 24 years old and, wanting to get involved in politics in some way, I called another political newcomer, Larry Stone, and volunteered to act as publicist for two city council candidates running on the ORCHARDS slate. Little did I realize that beyond the interviews and press releases, my last task would be to walk a precinct at 5 a.m. on election day stuffing flyers into screen doors while getting howled at by angry dogs. It was exhausting, but exhilarating as well. One of the two candidates won. Dianne McKenna is now a county supervisor. The loser, Dave Barram, did even better: He is now Undersecretary of Commerce.

The second story involves Fern Ohrt, who appears in these pages. During this same period, I got a call from the Sunnyvale Historical Society asking if I could do anything to help an elderly lady who was trying to save some downtown trees from being cleared for the new mall. It was just about the last thing I wanted to do, but I called her. What I encountered was a sweet old lady with a will of iron. The trees, Fern Ohrt said with unimpeachable certainty, were of great historic and sentimental importance — and though she attended one city council meeting after another to make her case, no one would listen to her. I wasn't a newspaperman yet, but I knew a good hook when I heard one. I wrote up as tearjerker a story as I could and sent it out under the historical society letterhead. I got the reporters there; Fern, who was as cagey as she was charming, did the rest: a front page story in the Palo Alto Times and the local section front of the San Jose Mercury News. In the end, the entire Sunnyvale Town Center was moved about fifty feet to accommodate the trees in their own climatically controlled atrium. And every time I pass them, I think about that indomitable old lady.

The final story involves my late father, Ralph "Pat" Malone, who also appears in this book. For this we have to go back to a Saturday morning in 1965. I was working on a merit badge, one of the requirements of which was to write about an historic site in my town. Living amidst a square mile of Eichlers, I didn't even know Sunnyvale had a history. But my father, always more enthusiastic about these projects than I was, learned of the location of the Martin Murphy house, one of the most important sites in the early history of California. Gulping down breakfast, we jumped in the car and raced over to see this legendary structure that had been shipped around the Horn to be the centerpiece of one of the greatest California land baronies.

What we found was a vacant lot choked with weeds and debris. The Murphy house had been bulldozed four years earlier.

My reaction was the typical shrug of an 11 year-old. But my father was furious. "How could they do that?" he kept asking on the long ride home. Within a few weeks, he had joined the Sunnyvale Historical Society. In time, this man who had never had a real home would become synony-mous with the history of Sunnyvale.

At the time, each of these people seemed quite normal to me. In retrospect I appreciate that they were all indeed special, if only in the way they rose to extraordinary times. The story of Sunnyvale is of just such people, genera-tion after generation, living out a dream of a new commu-nity.

Last year my wife, who also grew up here, and I moved back to our hometown. We bought the oldest surviv-ing house in Sunnyvale — the Wright House, built about 1855. It is not far from that fateful Silicon Valley intersection. Thus it spans the entire history of this city. And that is very important to us. Why? Because of my father and Fern Ohrt and all of the thousands of people who lived and died fulfilling the destiny of Sunnyvale.

Read this book and you'll understand.

MIKE MALONE
Sunnyvale, November 1993

INTRODUCTION

The City of Sunnyvale, best known today for its numerous high-technology and defense-related companies, occupies 25 square miles at the south western edge of San Francisco Bay. In 1750 the land lay virtually untouched by Western civilization. A mere two hundred years later, a technological revolution had its beginnings here. This book tells the story of Sunnyvale and its people, from the wealthy Irishman's estate on which a six-square-mile town was laid out, through the build-up of the fruit industry and the free-for-all annexations of unincorporated land in the 1950s and 1960s, to the major alterations of downtown and the birth of a high-technology enclave. The result is today's Sunnyvale, the "heart of Silicon Valley."

A one-time sheep pasture for grazing animals of Mission Santa Clara, Sunnyvale has evolved into a breeding ground of the computer age. Unfortunately, the people, places and events of the city's history are unknown to the vast majority of its present residents and workers. The cast of characters ranges from Ohlone Indian Chief Lopez Yñigo to local historian and tree preservationist Fern Ohrt, with all manner of personage in between. Even the street names conjure up personalities and places of the past: Murphy, Taaffe, Arques, Mathilda, Crossman, Hendy, Bay View, Carroll, Pastoria, and Borregas.

Sunnyvale was dubbed the "City of Destiny" by developer and founder Walter Crossman, probably more as a marketing ploy than any belief in a fate deigned by the gods.

The "destiny" rhetoric was proclaimed repeatedly throughout the city's history by financial and political promoters, and became a dominant theme at many turning points over the years. There can be a danger with the notion of "destiny," however, when it mitigates personal and collective responsibility for choices within the community.

In many ways, Sunnyvale's contemporary identity is as elusive and irregular as its city boundaries. They merge into neighboring cities with a sameness that does not clearly delineate the end of one city and the beginning of the next. This obscurity does not elicit a personal or historical connection with Sunnyvale. In part, this history is written out of a concern to recover hidden or lost identity so that residents feel a desire to participate in the community.

The history of Sunnyvale cannot be viewed in isolation from that of Santa Clara County, the San Francisco Bay Area, or even the whole of California. Factors that shaped the region also affected Sunnyvale, from the discovery of gold and the emergence of an agricultural economy, through the shift to war production and postwar population growth, to the technological revolution of the late twentieth century. Sunnyvale did not grow and develop in a vacuum, and it exemplifies some of the trends that have formed California as a whole. In this city's history, we can examine these large-scale historical developments at close range and explore their human dimensions.

The story of Sunnyvale has implications well beyond its boundaries. Other cities and towns have experienced significant change and rapid growth and although the specifics are different, we can draw conclusions and learn from one another's histories. Economic dependence on the military-industrial complex, the environmental impact of the technological age, and a growing sense of regional relationships are among the issues that must be addressed by Sunnyvale as well as many other American cities.

Reading Sunnyvale's history can also illuminate particular moments in time when decisions were made not made, which significantly impacted the town's futu There were some choices that we will find pleasing and source of pride; there are others that will disappoint anc disturb us. My hope is that this history will be a catalys the reader to participate in today's community in order create a better city whose citizens feel a real sense of loc history, thus engendering civic responsiblity and action.

Chapter 1

BEFORE SUNNYVALE: THE LAND AND THE PEOPLE

An occasional valley oak, a willow tree, or patches of marsh grasses near the edge of the bay are perhaps the only visible evidence of what today's Sunnyvale looked like 250 years ago. Most of the huge, ancient oak trees that dominated the scene were removed by fruit farmers. Gone are the tule reed marshes, the willow groves and chaparral grasses that offered sustenance to hundreds of species of geese, pelicans, quail, eagles and giant condors. Gone are the herds of wild game that roamed the land, the grizzlies, elk, antelope, deer, and the smaller wolves, foxes and rabbits.[1]

The indigenous people were described by the Spanish explorers as "the coast dwellers," thus named costanos or Costanoans, although subsequent generations have preferred to be called Ohlone. The abundance of the San Francisco Bay environment supported relatively stable, non-competitive village communities with ample food from natural vegetation, wild game or small animals. Shellfish were the basis for their diet, however, and burial sites at nearby surviving shell mounds provide clues to how native people lived their daily lives. A 1972 excavation from the Sunnyvale East Drainage Channel yielded a human skeleton, "Sunnyvale girl," dating from the middle holocene age, approximately 3,500 to 5,000 years ago.[2] A Native American "charm stone" was also found in Sunnyvale near the north end of Borregas Avenue. A large village, Posolmi, was

Sketch of Mission Santa Clara drawn in 1851 after the Jesuits established a college at the site of the Mission. Original sketch is in the Californiana Collection, Jesuit Archives, Rome, Italy. Courtesy Santa Clara University Archives.

located where Moffett Field stands today. Villagers from Posolmi gathered food and hunted game on the land which is Sunnyvale. They lived here for hundreds of years before the arrival of the Spanish, using only what they needed, having very little permanent impact on the land.[3]

Spanish explorers arrived in California in the 1770s, established military installations and missions and forced the native population to labor in European systems of trade and agriculture, resulting in the abandonment of native villages. The Spanish misinterpreted the natives' way of life as uncivilized and idolatrous and set about to transform it. The result was a clash of cultures, ending in the dominance of one over the other — the first in a series of such clashes that would occur here over the next two centuries.

Natives of the Sunnyvale area were drafted to work at Mission Santa Clara, founded by Spanish Franciscan missionaries on January 12, 1777. In 1800, the Indians at Mission Santa Clara numbered 2,228, which was more than any of the other missions.[4] They labored in agricultural endeavors growing grapes, pears, figs and grain while cattle and sheep grazed in pastures to the northeast of the mission proper, in an area the Spanish named *la pastoria de las borregas* (literally, ewe lambs pasture). The pasture would be marked off as a rancho in the 1840s, named *Rancho Pastoria de las Borregas*, and eventually renamed Sunnyvale. Within the first twenty years of Spanish settlement, the native villages of the Sunnyvale area were completely depopulated. The Indians who survived epidemics of European diseases lived at Mission Santa Clara, converted to Christianity willingly or not, and labored for the mission and the Spanish Crown.

The padres' primary motivation was to convert the natives to Christianity, while the main goal of the military was to claim the territory for Spain and increase trade to accumulate wealth. The padres planned to hold all the land until such time that the natives could farm and trade in the Spanish tradition, an estimated ten years. Spain would give land back to Christianized natives, who would then be Spanish citizens and provide protection from incursion by

other nations attempting to colonize California. Unlike the English colonists on the Eastern coast of North America who never gave serious consideration to assimilating the native populations into their own, the Spanish sought to convert natives to Catholicism, the Spanish economic system and language, as well as to intermarry. Marriage between the Spanish and Indians was more common than between the English and Indians primarily because there were so few Spanish women willing to venture to New Spain and Alta California. In both cases, however, the native cultures were destroyed.

From the very beginning there was conflict between the padres and the military on what means ought to be used to achieve Spain's various goals. The missions functioned not only as farms, but also as mini-manufactories of leather goods, woven cloth, tools and wines. The successful, self-sufficient ventures were regarded jealously by those at the presidios who had to depend for survival on the arrival of supply ships or on the bounty of the missions where the padres exercised economic as well as spiritual control. It became increasingly clear that Spain was simply too far away from the Americas to enforce effective policies. These conflicts were never resolved and ended only with secularization. Mission lands and labor forces were usurped by the civilian and military leaders.[5]

In 1821, after forty years of relative isolation because Spain was embroiled in so many conflicts at home, an independent Mexican Republic took control of present-day Mexico, Texas, Arizona, New Mexico and California. With secularization, Spanish-born padres were expelled, trade regulations were relaxed, and an era of new land tenure systems began.

The new Mexican government attempted to strengthen its grasp on the area by granting large tracts of land, including mission properties, to persons of Spanish or Mexican heritage who resided in California, or *Californios* as they came to be called. Previously unable to own land because they were not pure Spanish and of the highest class *gente de razon* (people of reason), many *Californios* applied for and were granted large tracts of property. The power base in California shifted from Franciscan missionaries and Spanish governors to *Californio* ranchero families. Native Americans had no means of support, and in most cases, no ancestral village awaiting their return. They were left with very little choice but to attempt to find a surviving group of natives or work as vaqueros and ranch hands on the ranchos of the *Californios*.

Two land grants from California governors involved the land of present-day Sunnyvale. *Rancho Posolmi* was one of a few parcels of land granted to an Indian. Chief Lupe (sometimes Lopez) Yñigo, received almost 1,700 acres in 1844 from Governor Micheltorena. The area had been the site of the Posolmi tribal village where present-day Moffett Field stands, located to the north of *Rancho Pastoria de las Borregas*.

Yñigo was born to local Indians and had been christened at Mission Santa Clara. After the breakup of the mission lands, Yñigo went back to his ancestral land where he built an abobe which he shared with his family and other Indians. By the 1840s, Yñigo was well-known to the local ranchero families, and his farm was well established. It is perhaps for this reason that Governor Micheltorena issued a land grant to him. In the 1850s, there were at least seventeen

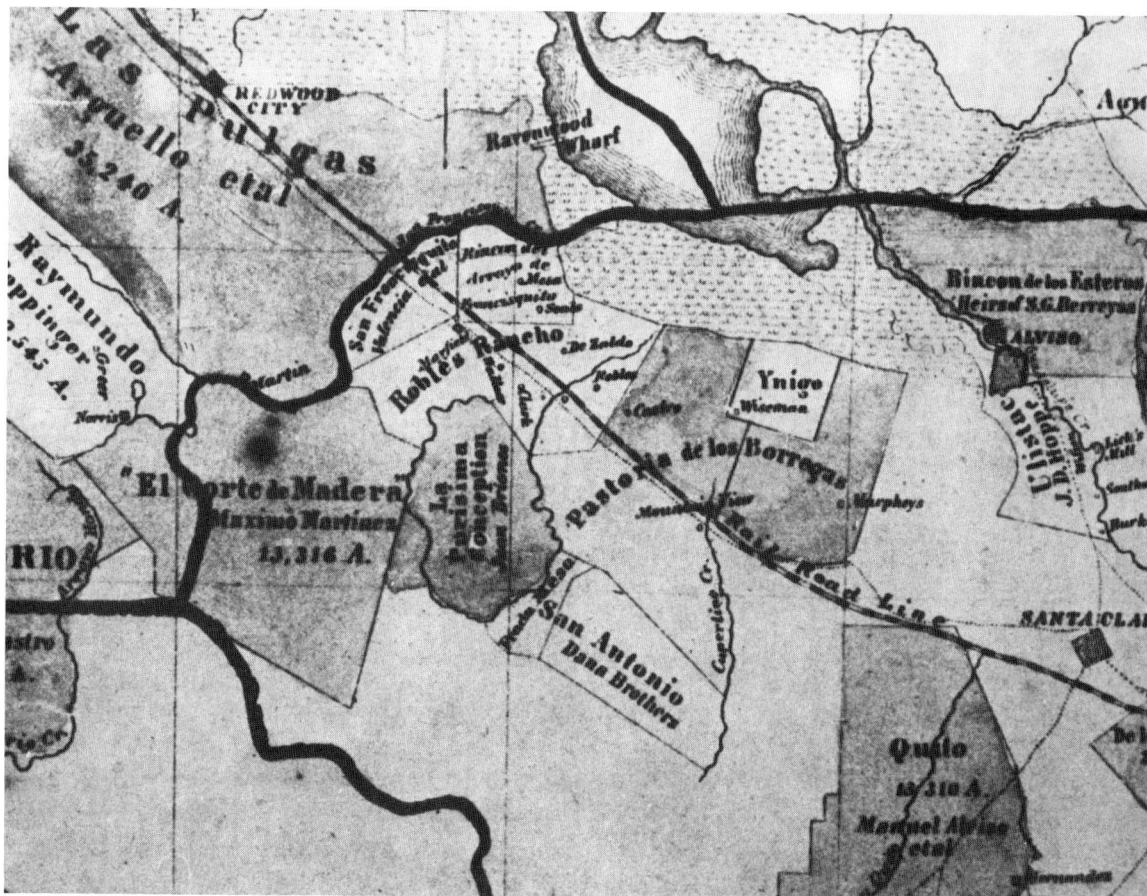

Map showing Rancho Yñigo and Rancho Pastoria de las Borregas, circa 1870. Courtesy California History Center, Stocklmeir Library/ Archives.

others living with Yñigo on the rancho, including his "squaw." They grew wheat and barley, and owned cows, horses and sheep. This rancho functioned self-sufficiently, in the tradition of the mission economic and agricultural systems on which Yñigo had been raised.

A glimpse of Yñigo's personality is possible because of contemporary accounts describing him. Alfred Doten, an

Lupe (Lopez) Yñigo, native Californian raised at Mission Santa Clara who was granted Rancho Posolmi later referred to as Rancho Yñigo. Courtesy Santa Clara University Archives.

Alf Doten whose voluminous journals describe people, places and events in the West. Courtesy University of Nevada, Reno, Doten Collection.

eccentric New Englander who had come to California in search of gold, wrote meticulous daily entries in his diary, carefully describing places he went and characters he encountered. Doten's entries during the 1850s shed light on many aspects of early Santa Clara County since he worked as a ranch hand in Mountain View. He described one conversation with Yñigo this way:

> Sunday, April 11 [1858]
> *When I went up this morning, old Ynego (sic) rode up*

with me, as far as M. V. [Mountain View] — the old fellow says when he was a little boy, his tribe was numerous about here — but all have died, and he is the only one left — says the bears were there — very numerous all through the woods, and they killed lots of Indians — says he thinks God sent the bears to kill all bad Christians — lucky there are no bears here nowadays —[6]

Doten's tongue-in-cheek reference to his own lapsed Christianity typifies his sense of humor throughout his voluminous journal. Doten also recalled his frustrated attempt to have Yñigo's wife wash his laundry:

> January 5 [1857]
> *took the washing along, but not being able to find anyone to do it, I had to leave it at old Indigo's (sic) for his squaw to wash — Sunset, I was up to Indigo's and his squaw told me she could not do it because she has 'a picaniny in her belly,' so I had to take the bundle back home.*[7]

"Old" Yñigo must have been fathering children as late as 1857. The rancho subsequently became known as *Rancho Yñigo*, and the old Indian eventually sold portions of the property to support himself and his family. When he died, however, the remaining land did not pass to any Indian heirs but was patented in 1881 to the Walkinshaw family, whose claims to the area were upheld in court.

The area which today is Sunnyvale was part of *Rancho Pastoria de las Borregas*. In 1842, California Governor Juan Bautista Alvarado of Mexico honored a request by Mariano Castro and granted an 8,800-acre parcel to Francisco Estrada and his wife Inez (Castro), Mariano's daughter. El Camino Real was the southern border of the grant, which ran from today's Lawrence Expressway to Castro Street in Mountain View. The Castros were descended from Spaniards in Mexico who accompanied Juan Bautista de Anza on his second expedition in 1775-76 overland from Sinaloa to

San Francisco. The family became prominent in California, and Mariano was named *alcalde* (magistrate or mayor) of San José in 1828 and 1830. Mariano married Maria Trinidad Peralta, thereby aligning two powerful ranchero families in the Bay Area. They had nine children, among them Inez, Merced (Castro) Calderon, Josefa (Castro) Davidson, and Crisanto Castro. Inez and Francisco Estrada died within a short time of each other and the property went to Francisco's father, José Mariano Estrada. He died shortly thereafter, and the land grant reverted to Mariano Castro.[8] The Castro family built an adobe and moved onto the property in 1843, and their house was located in what is now Mountain View. The Castros raised cattle on the land through the 1840s, but the impact of the gold rush ultimately led them to sell most of the property.

The flood of Euro-Americans who migrated to California after the discovery of gold began as a trickle in the early 1840s. Among the few hundred people arriving from points east of the Mississippi was Martin Murphy, Jr., an Irish-born immigrant, who pioneered from Missouri over the Sierra Nevada to California as part of the Stephens party with his father, brothers and their families in 1844. The Stephens-Murphy party preceded the ill-fated Donner expedition and their courageous adventure indicates the depth of their desire to go West.

Martin Murphy, Jr. had married Mary Bolger, also a native of Ireland, in Quebec in 1831. Their first children were born in Canada where they remained until 1842 when they joined the senior Murphy family in "Irish Grove," Missouri. After a brief, unhappy period in epidemic-ridden Missouri where three of Mary and Martin's daughters died along with his mother, the remaining Murphy clan set out for California in search of a good farming climate and a place to comfortably practice Catholicism. The caravan, led by Elisha Stephens, made its way West and became the first wagon train to successfully negotiate the Sierra Nevada mountain range. The trek began on May 18, 1844 and it was a full year before the entire group was settled in California. Martin and Mary brought their four sons, James, Martin III, Patrick Washington, and Bernard Daniel, on the trek across the desert and over the Sierras. The expedition must have been particularly grueling for Mary Murphy, pregnant all the while with daughter Elizabeth Yuba Murphy who was born when they reached California while the party was camped on the Yuba River. Family stories tell that as the Murphys traversed the Yuba River on horseback, their new infant daughter, Lizzie, slipped from her mother's saddle into the icy water. Martin snatched her quickly from the foamy current, later adding "Yuba" to her name to commemorate her untimely baptism.[9]

Settlers who arrived in California before the gold rush formed a loose community of friendship and support to help each other survive. John Sutter's fort, at what is today Sacramento, was a welcome sight to many of the arrivals, and the Murphys were no exception. Martin and his father Martin, Sr. and brothers, Daniel, Patrick, and John were cajoled into joining Sutter's mini-army in support of Governor Micheltorena. Sutter listed the Murphy men in his diary as participants in skirmishes leading to the Bear Flag Revolt and noted:

> *Roster of the Forces Which Left Sutter's Fort January First, 1845 . . . The little army marched [to San Jose under Captain Gantt] to the aid of Governor Manuel Micheltorena and against the revolting Californians under Jose Castro and former Governor Juan Bautista Alvarado.*[10]

LEFT:
Martin Murphy, Jr.

RIGHT:
Mary Bolger Murphy

It was months before they returned to the banks of the Yuba River to rejoin their families.

While Martin Murphy, Sr. went on to the Santa Clara Valley and bought land near San José, the junior Martin Murphy purchased land from Ernest Rufus in the Cosumnes River region of the Sacramento Valley about fifteen miles from Sutter's fort for $250 and successfully grew wheat and raised cattle. Like many early European and American arrivals, they were successful farmers when gold was discovered at Sutter's mill. The steady stream of gold seekers became a source of great wealth for those like Murphy who were ready to provide wheat, beef, horses, supplies and lodging to the arriving masses. The Murphy ranch, like Sutter's fort, was a popular stopping place for those pioneers just arriving in California from the East. Explorer and diarist Bayard Taylor recorded his impressions while lodging with the Martin Murphy, Jr. family at the Consumnes River ranch:

> Mr. Murphy, I found, was the son of the old gentleman whose hospitalities I had shared in the valley of San Jose. He had been living three years on the river, and his three sturdy young sons could ride and throw the lariat equal to any Californian. There were two or three Indian boys belonging to the house, one of whom, a solid, shock-headed urchin, as grave as if he was born to be a "medicine-man," did all the household duties with great precision and steadiness. He was called "Billy," and though he understood English as well as his own language, I never heard him speak.[11]

Like other ranchero families in California, the Murphy's domestic help was Native American. By 1880 however, the domestic workers at the Murphys had Irish surnames.[12]

Euro-Americans who sought to own property in California were required either to swear allegiance to Mexico by becoming a Mexican citizen and converting to Catholicism or by marrying a *Californio* woman. On January 28, 1846, Murphy applied for and was granted Mexican citizenship to ensure his rights to the Consumnes River

property.[13] He and other newcomers sided with Governor Micheltorena because they felt their claims to property were more likely to be honored than by former Governor Alvarado.

In June of 1846, Lieutenant Francisco Arce, an emissary of former governor Alvarado and therefore a supposed enemy of Murphy's, camped at Murphy's Consumnes River ranch with his men and horses. While they were on Murphy's property, the Lieutenant and his horses were taken captive by some other settlers. Thus began the war between Mexico and those favoring a California republic. Interestingly, Arce's captivity was shortlived and Martin Murphy, Jr. allowed him to leave with his men, some horses and supplies. Thomas O. Larkin, the consul of the United States in Monterey, noted the incident in this way:

> From April to June the foreigners in the Sacramento Valley, were continually harassed by verbal reports & written proclamations, that they must leave California. The first week of June, Lieutenant Francisco Arce, with eleven soldiers in bringing 170 horses & mares belonging to his General, Castro, then at Headquarters, Santa Clara Mission, had to cross the Sacramento near New Helvetia. One morning while eating at their camp fires at the house of Martin Murphy of Ireland, was visited by one Merritt an American, one O'Farlen (Irish) and ten other foreigners, who demanded their guns & horses, which without resistance were given up. Lieut. Arce & party were then allowed their arms, the horses under the saddle & and a fresh horse each.[14]

Ironically, even though Murphy was supposedly on the opposing side, he evidently maintained a longterm relationship with Francisco Arce, which included loaning him $200 at 2% interest in 1860. Martin Murphy's Consumnes River ranch is designated today by historical landmark as the site of the first overt action of the Mexican-American War.

In 1850, with the war over, and California a part of

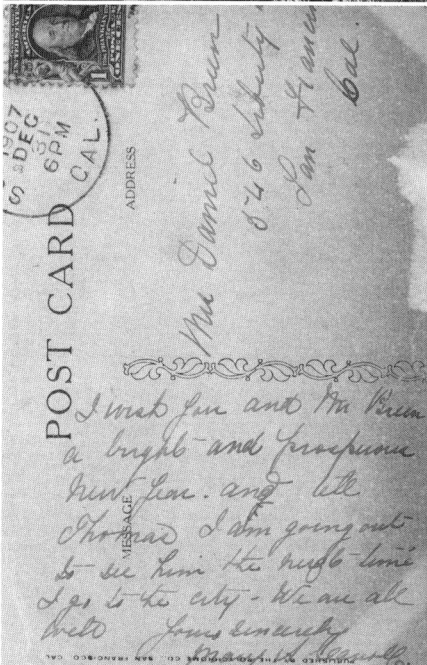

Postcard depicting "Bay View" sent as a New Year's greeting by Murphy daughter Mary Ann Carroll, 1907. By this time, the house was already fifty-seven years old. Picture postcards of personal residences were very popular at the turn of the century. Courtesy Sunnyvale Historical Society & Museum Association

chased rather than swindled, the change in ownership in this rancho typifies some clashes that occurred between *Californios* and Euro-Americans. Given the political climate in California, it is unlikely that Mariano Castro or his heirs would have been able to maintain physical or financial control of 8,800 acres for very long. After the purchase, Murphy moved his entire family to the Santa Clara Valley for a number of reasons, among them its superior climate, his desire to be near his father and brothers living in San José, and a growing frustration at the thievery and lawlessness in the Sacramento area resulting from the gold rush.[15]

By the time Martin Murphy, Jr. moved to the Santa Clara Valley he was already a wealthy man. In 1850, he received $50,000 for three thousand head of cattle and half of the property he had purchased six years earlier for $250. Murphy had the wherewithal to order a prefabricated frame house from a lumber mill in New England and have it sent by ship around Cape Horn to be reconstructed on the recently acquired property. It was the first frame house in Santa Clara County and the Murphy family renamed the Rancho "Bay View" for its unobstructed view of the southern part of San Francisco Bay. Surrounding the house,

> the garden, patio in design, was fragrant with
> Castilian roses, jessamine, passion vines, pomegranate
> and pepper trees. A second garden embraced great oak
> and fig trees. Planted by one of the Franciscan padres,
> there still stands a magnificent fig tree, whose
> branches have spread, descended and rooted so that
> under it eighty people can now find shelter.[16]

Their status grew and they became very well known in social and political circles in the Santa Clara Valley.

Once again Alf Doten's prolific journal gives us a glimpse of social affairs in the early years at Murphy's Bay View. Doten's expertise as a fiddle player garnered him many invitations:

> Two of the Murphy boys came to see me, to get me to
> come and play for them tomorrow night at their house,

the United States, the junior Martin Murphy visited San José to purchase cattle for resale in the mining regions. The cattle seller refused the price Murphy offered, however, and somewhat impulsively, Murphy used the cash he was carrying to pay Mariano Castro the sum of $12,500 for a portion of *Rancho Pastoria de las Borregas*. Two smaller additional tracts of land were purchased after United States Land Commission rulings in the 1850s, for a combined total of 4,800 acres. Although *Pastoria de las Borregas* was pur-

Interior of Murphy home, circa 1906. Some of the furnishings such as the candlesticks, piano and portrait are presently in the collection of the Sunnyvale Historical Museum. Courtesy Sunnyvale Historical Society & Museum Association.

as they are going to have a dancing party . . . .
There were some 30 or 40 men present, but only
seven women, including Mrs. M and the servant
girl (Hannah O'Rourke). The showers, and
threatening appearance of the weather prevented
any more ladies from being present — We had a very
jolly time — Cotillions, reels, waltzes, jigs, polkas and
other figures without number were danced. Mrs.
Murphy and Mrs. Lacy, with two gentlemen,
showed us how the Irish jig was performed . . . .
About 5 1/2 o'clock in the morning the ball broke up,
and some of the ladies left.[17]

Mary and Martin Murphy, Jr. had eleven children. Three daughters, Eliza, Mary and Nellie, died in Missouri. Eldest son James died in 1852 at age twenty at Bay View on the same day Mary Murphy gave birth to his youngest brother, also named James. The Murphy children grew to adulthood at Bay View, the girls attending Notre Dame College while the boys were educated at Santa Clara College. They eventually became prominent citizens in the San Francisco Bay Area.

Martin Murphy III married Susan Maguire, but he

Bernard Murphy (right) who went on to become mayor of San José and Robert Keating while students at Santa Clara College, circa 1860. Courtesy Santa Clara University Archives.

died as a young man in 1865. Patrick W. Murphy was elected a state senator and became known as "General Murphy," the state's first Adjutant General. Bernard D. Murphy, familiarly called "Barney," was a lawyer who served three times as Mayor of San José, as well as serving as state senator and a member of the state legislature. He was one of the founders of Lick Observatory on Mount Hamilton. The second James became the first bank commissioner for the state of California and served as state senator.

The Murphy daughters were as socially prominent

as their brothers were politically. Elizabeth Yuba Murphy married William Taaffe and they were given 2,800 acres, part of today's Foothill College, as a wedding gift. Both Elizabeth and William died while their children were underage, and the youngsters were raised by their grandparents, Mary and Martin Murphy, Jr. at Bay View. Mary Ann Murphy married San Franciscan Richard Carroll, and Ellen (Nellie) Murphy married Spanish-born Santa Claran Joaquin Arques who died in 1882.

Like many other large landowners in California, Martin Murphy, Jr. molded Bay View into a vast wheat-producing estate and cattle ranch more as a speculative venture than to create a self-sufficient family farm. In 1852, fewer than 145,000 acres were producing wheat in the state. The average price per bushel was $2.40, with the average planted acre yielding twenty bushels. By 1861, the price per bushel had fallen to less than half of what it had been ten years earlier, but the number of acres planted swelled to over 361,000. Growing wheat became much more competitive, but Murphy was able to maximize profits because he imported the most efficient farm equipment from the East via Panama. According to his son, Bernard, Murphy was also the first to import Norman horses to California. Like several other land barons in the state, he did not regret the demise of the *Californios* and used cheap labor provided by Chinese and Native Americans. With the profits realized from his ranch, he bought more real estate in several counties.

The 1850s were particularly turbulent in California because of raging land ownership disputes between *Californios*, Euro-American settlers, and squatters. The Land Commission Act of 1851 was passed by the federal government to establish a commission to determine the validity of Mexican land titles. By virtue of the Treaty of Guadalupe-Hidalgo, which signalled the end of the Mexican-American War, the grants of the Mexican government were supposed to remain intact. The grantees had to prove title, however, which took on average, a grueling seventeen years.[18] Many property owners did not live long enough to get through court battles, and for others, the cost of litigation was completely overwhelming. Most had to sell property in order to pay legal fees.

Martin Murphy, Jr. had the resources to successfully prove title to thousands of acres. His main problem, however, like many other landowners, was dealing with squatters: those settlers who staked out a homestead on property already owned by another. Shelvy Kifer, a recent arrival from the East, settled his family on a portion of Murphy's land, although Kifer claimed he thought it was government property. Kifer and other squatters viewed themselves as settlers, willing to build and improve the land. They posed a threat to the wealth of Murphy and others like him, however, and were not tolerated. Murphy pursued legal action against the squatters, and as Alf Doten noted "Murphy is fencing up the Northerly side of the Alviso road — fine stout fence. . . His lawsuit has turned out successful, and Ralston, Norato, Charley Worthington, [illegible] and the others all have to leave."[19]

By 1860, Martin Murphy, Jr. owned real estate valued at $60,000 with $60,000 worth of personal property,[20] and during the next decade, he purchased three contiguous ranchos in San Luis Obispo County: Santa Margarita, Atascadero, and Asuncion. The seller, Joaquin Estrada, was forced to sell because his attempts to prove title involved extended litigation. Murphy bought the land from third parties who foreclosed on the Estrada ranchos. The Irishman's business dealings led him to hold $2 million in real estate,[21] and at one point, he owned 90,000 acres in several counties, making him one of the wealthiest men in the state. Only 3,000 acres were actively farmed in any given year, however, and the remainder was grazing land for vast herds of cattle and horses.[22]

In 1861 Murphy issued a "Release of Right of Way" to the San Francisco and San José Railroad to lay track on his property, provided they would pick up passengers from "Murphy Station," as the flagstop became popularly known. Later, he paid $2,000 to build Lawrence Station, at the south end of Bay View which was named for Albert C. Lawrence, founder of that tiny community in the 1850s. With the decline of goldmining and the completion of the transcontinental railroad, thousands of Chinese were forced out of Mother Lode and Comstock towns. Many came to the Santa Clara Valley to build the San Francisco-San José rail link and then became farm laborers. Perhaps one of the real keys to Murphy's wealth as well as that of other large California landowners, rested in his use of cheap labor, among them the Chinese who were not legally eligible to own land. By 1870, at least twelve Chinese farm laborers who owned neither land nor personal property lived in an outbuilding at Bay View.[23]

The Chinese had a major impact on the economy of the valley because they built the railroad and subsequently became farm laborers. Anti-Chinese campaigns throughout the San Francisco Bay Area by groups like the Workingman's Party, of which Bernard Murphy was a member, were beginning to be successful in limiting the number of Chinese in the area. Nevertheless, in 1880 the Chinese made up 48.2% of the farm labor force in Santa Clara County and through 1900, despite an end to Chinese immigration with the Chinese Exclusion Act in 1882, there were a substantial number of Chinese in the Sunnyvale area. The exclusion laws, along with the fact that there were almost no Chinese women, made the Chinese population drop precipitously after 1900.

Nothing expresses the breadth of the wealth and prestige of the Murphy family quite like the story of the celebration of the fiftieth wedding anniversary of Mary and Martin Murphy, Jr.[24] The Murphy children wanted to plan a party in their parents' honor, and judging from Alf Doten's remarks, among others, this was a family with a long tradition of parties. Rather than invite specific guests, the elderly Martin instructed his sons to issue a general invitation in area newspapers. In July 1881 they released an open invitation to a giant barbecue at Bay View in honor of the Murphy's fiftieth wedding anniversary. The San Francisco Examiner claimed "it is the desire of the happy and generous old couple and their family that all may come who will, as

the Murphy rancho will keep 'open house' for the entire surrounding country." The expected 3,000 swelled to a supposed 10,000 guests,[25] and not surprisingly since Barney Murphy was mayor, city offices and superior court in San José closed because judges, attorneys, and public officials flocked to the party. Trains carried guests from San Francisco and San José to Murphy Station where they were greeted by an eighteen-piece band, heartily playing "Come Haste to the Wedding." By one count, eight hundred carriages and wagons clambered to the ranch, delivering friends, family and even complete strangers to the much ballyhooed social event of the century.

Each of the Murphy children and their spouses were assigned specific tasks in the management of the colossal affair. The eldest, Patrick, was the general manager while youngest son, James was in charge of greeting the guests upon their arrival. Dick Carroll, Mary Ann's husband, was rightly assigned to the liquor detail since he owned an alcohol distribution company in San Francisco. Reports claimed it took an entire rail car to carry kegs, bottles and lagers to the party site. Son-in-law Joaquin Arques directed the actual barbecue and hired renowned culinary king Isaac Branham and a fellow named Smith to prepare the food. A week earlier preparations had begun when a huge trench had been dug, and two days ahead they began to burn the seven cords of wood it took to create glowing coals to roast the meat. The fires were tended by "Negroes and Mexicans" while Branham roasted fourteen sheep, ten pigs, and seven steer on metal rods hanging over the hundred-foot-long trench. The chef basted the carcasses with a butter-soaked mop "with the care that an artist applies the finishing touches to his exhibition painting." Smoked hams and roasted chickens were also presented with one thousand loaves of bread accompanied by hundreds of pounds of salad tossed from bushel baskets. And of course no Irish feast is complete without libation of lemonade, beer, claret and whiskey aplenty for all.

Bay View's oak grove was decorated with hanging Chinese lanterns to illuminate the festivities. Tables were set

The first frame house in Santa Clara County, Martin Murphy, Jr.'s "Bay View". Photo shows additions to original structure. Courtesy Sunnyvale Historical Society & Museum Association.

and a large dancing platform was erected and minstrels wandered, giving honor to the elderly couple who had such an influence throughout the county. Even a bagpiper entertained, harkening back to the celtic past of many of the party goers. Several prominent guests offered tributes and toasts including Senators William Gwin and James Phelan, while Murphy children read notes of congratulations from longtime friends Archbishop Alemany and Governor Perkins. A few guests had been travelers with the Murphys in their trek of the 1840s, including Moses Schallenberger, Dennis Martin, and Martin Murphy Jr.'s brothers, Daniel and John Murphy.

The spectacular barbecue contributed mightily to the "rags to riches" mythology which surrounded the Murphy family. Fueled by their pioneering trek across the Sierra Nevada, their financial success in California after meager immigrant beginnings, their philanthropic contributions to Santa Clara College and Notre Dame, and topped off with the gargantuan barbecue, the Murphy myth has been perpetuated and embellished to include numerous virtues. It is also clear, however, based on census manuscripts, court records, and contemporary diaries that Murphy capitalized on cheap labor, purchased properties from those in severe financial straits, and aggressively litigated against squatters.

Murphy biographer Sister Gabrielle Sullivan, the only one to chronicle the life of this important and powerful 19th-century Californian, asserts that Murphy "had no part in the gold rush."

> *Conservative in outlook, Murphy had no part in the gold rush or resulting speculation. However, the qualities of an astute business man helped him to utilize to his advantage the existing conditions in the mining section of the state.*[26]

While it may be true that Murphy did not actually pan for gold himself, his wealth can be directly attributed to his earnings while supplying gold miners with beef, wheat and lodging. Even diarist Bayard Taylor recalled the oft-men- tioned "Murphy hospitality" that he encountered on the Consumnes River ranch. Interestingly enough, Taylor did not complain that the hospitality cost him and others who stayed there $4.00 per night, quite a sum for 1849.[27]

Authors Timothy Lukes and Gary Okihiro, in their book Japanese Legacy, suggest that "families like the Murphy's dominated the economic and political life of the valley during the 1850s, creating a landed aristocracy and instituting a system of paternalism."[28] Murphy, one of the largest landowners in California, appears to have become a part of precisely what his family had fled in English-domi- nated Ireland: a landed gentry controlling the lives of tenant farmers. Historian Paul Gates goes so far as to say "The Murphys, father and son, skimmed the cream off the land, created a small fortune for themselves through extensive use, but incurred for themselves much ill will for their treatment of settlers."[29] Although some of Murphy's policies toward hired help or squatters were less than exemplary by late 20th-century standards, his attitudes were typical of his era.

Nineteenth-century historians recorded the most positive attributes of the prominent people that they pro- filed. When Hubert Howe Bancroft compiled his Chronicles of the Builders of the Commonwealth (1891), a letter from William McQuoid urged him to impress Bernard Murphy with the biographical sketch of Martin Murphy, Jr.:

> *Please remember that the Hon. B. D. Murphy is the person who we especially want to please. In addition to the dictation and biography cited, he is now a candidate on the Cleveland ticket for elector at large, having been nominated without any knowledge or effort on his part.*
>
> *He is the business successor of his father. By unanimous consent he is said to be just like his father in liberality and manly principles.*
>
> *I want you to say as little as possible about the brothers and sisters of Martin Murphy Jun [sic] Let whatever may be said, be of a complimentary character.*[30]

Clearly Bancroft's version of the Murphy family story is a carefully edited one.

Martin Murphy died in 1884 and his estate, estimated in value between three and five million dollars, was divided among his children and grandchildren. Martin and Mary had deeded their properties to their children while they were still living to simplify their estate. Their only stipulation had been that they keep the income of their holdings until their death. The heirs included sons Bernard D. Murphy, James T. Murphy, Patrick W. Murphy, and the Murphy daughters Mrs. Nellie G. Arques and Mrs. Mary Ann Carroll. Each received 820 acres of property, much of which they leased out to tenant farmers. The four orphaned children of Elizabeth Yuba Murphy and William Taaffe, William, Martin, Mathilda and Mary received 820 acres among them. The Bay View property directly surrounding the Murphy house was managed for all by Bernard Murphy while Patrick Murphy managed and lived on the land in San Luis Obispo County. Most of the property was not divided and sold until after Mary Murphy's death in 1892.

The death of Martin Murphy, Jr. in 1884 coincided with a decline in the viability of California wheat production and the beginning of a shift toward smaller landowners in the Santa Clara Valley. Several factors contributed to the sale of large tracts of land and their division into smaller parcels. For one thing, other patriarchs of the wealthiest families in the valley died, and their landholdings were divided among heirs or sold. For the most part, they sold the smaller parcels to immigrants from southern European countries who made up a growing mercantile class. Second, most of the disputed land titles resulting from the Mexican-American War were settled in the 1870s and 1880s and those who had previously been unable to sell because of a clouded title were now free to do so.

Wheat farming declined as financial incentives dwindled by the 1880s. Competition from the Mississippi Valley and Russia exacerbated the situation and it also became clear that wheat farming depleted the soil. Land that had previously produced four or five crops in a single season, yielded half that by the 1880s. Livestock trade that accompanied wheat farming was dealt serious blows by the drought in 1864 and new California enclosure laws. The regulations stipulated that adjoining landowners could press charges for damage resulting from roaming animals and thieves would not be prosecuted unless fencing was installed.

At the same time that wheat and cattle ranchers experienced financial pressures, a property tax introduced in Santa Clara County in the 1870s also encouraged the breakup of huge landholdings. Properties were assessed whether or not they were actively producing. Only small portions of very large estates, like Murphy's, were planted and harvested each year. Tax payments on hundreds of idle acres were a drain on the cash flow of landowners.[31] Even though the value of Murphy's estate was estimated from three to five million dollars, the annual income was rumored as only $60,000, which could account for the sale of the bulk of the estate in the 1890s.[32]

The San José Board of Trade (later the chamber of commerce) reorganized in 1886 and, along with Santa Clara County officials, actively sought to populate the county to expand the economy with commerce generated by newcomers. Promotional pamphlets generated by the board of trade, proclaimed the "Garden of the World," an idyllic Eden of bountiful fruit trees and vines laden with grapes. These pamphlets were at least partially responsible for drawing settlers to the valley. The county recorder hired extra clerks to process the mountain of paperwork generated by increased land sales and by mid-1886, land values were doubling every thirty days.

Not long before, William Wright and his wife built their two-story farm house not far from the Murphy ranch. Wright, a Maryland native, had come to California seeking his fortune in gold, and over time, became a successful farmer in Santa Clara County. The stately old house today is the oldest building in Sunnyvale, and although the tank house has been relocated on the property, both structures have been designated with landmark status.[33]

George Briggs, a Bostonian who had come to California in 1850 and sought "a squatters claim" near today's Hollenbeck and Fremont avenues gave a lecture to the Santa Clara County Pioneers in 1895 in which he described the look of his land when he first arrived:

> The improvements on the farm consisted of a cabin 12 feet square, and a brush fence enclosing 7 acres. The cabin was under a large live oak tree. I have since built on another part of my place and the old oak still stands, and frequently when I pass beneath its wide spreading branches, my mind goes back to the old times when I lived beneath its shelter. I look at the old tree and thinking of the many changes in its surroundings, I admire it.[34]

Briggs turned his land into orchards and aligned himself with New Yorker William Hollenbeck, who purchased adjacent land. Hollenbeck's daughter married George Briggs, which also helped the two families to join forces against incursion by other squatters. Just after the turn of the century, a fellow named Henry Stelling bought the Briggs land.

The look of the land changed dramatically. What had been wheat fields became orchards. The average size of farms in Santa Clara County declined substantially between 1880 and 1900. In the mid-1880s, there were roughly 700 Santa Clara County farms over one hundred acres and 700 under one hundred acres. In 1890, 1,400 county farms had fewer than one hundred acres, while 750 farms had more. By the turn of the century, over 3,000 farms in Santa Clara County were smaller than one hundred acres and 938 were larger.[35]

The changes in land use were accentuated by the development of new business ventures that encouraged fruit production. In 1871, James and Eloise Dawson established the first cannery in Santa Clara County, initially out of the kitchen of their farm on The Alameda, and later on a larger scale. Other local canneries opened, primarily to compete with San Francisco canners. The emerging canning industry in the valley kept the demand for fruit high and encouraged farmers to plant more trees. Fruit drying gained popularity with the discovery that a sulphur additive made the sun more effective at drying fruit than costly evaporators. The introduction of the refrigerated rail car in 1888 also made fruit growing a more viable endeavor. Fruit orcharding and the canning industry grew up virtually side by side, establishing a symbiotic relationship which lasted until the next century when orchards and fruit production were eliminated by residential and industrial land development.

The arrival of Southern European immigrants to the valley reinforced the changes in the land. Louis and Pierre Pellier, Paul Masson, and Pierre Mirassou were among those who brought with them an expertise in fruit and vine growing. They capitalized on the natural availability of water and farmers like George Briggs developed effective irrigation systems for their crops. Lemuel and Salvin Collins bought 160 acres and planted grapes, making their own spirits at their distillery which still stands on today's Cascade Drive. Later their vines succumbed to phylloxera (root louse) and the land was replanted with fruit trees. All these factors contributed to the development of fruit production in California in general, and Santa Clara County in particular. The state agricultural society journals from the 1880s say that wheat production would not have sustained the state's economy as it had in the past, but vineyards and orchards saved the state's agricultural industry from ruin.[36]

The former Murphy ranch and surrounding area began to become more heavily populated by families establishing orchards and farms. In 1881, Rolla and Emma Butcher, he of Virginia and she an English immigrant, bought a 160-acre oak-dotted hayfield near what is today's Wolfe Road and El Camino Real. Rolla died shortly after arriving, but Emma planted fruit trees like many other farmers in the valley and managed the property herself. She was one of only three women farmers at the 1886 Fruit Growers' convention held in Sacramento. Although she was forced to sell bits of land, just barely escaping foreclosure, she farmed successfully and raised three children on her orchard property that became known locally as "Butcher's Corners."[37]

In the 1890s, Charles Morse of Santa Clara leased 1,400 acres on the former Murphy ranch for his Morse seed-growing operation. Morse Avenue was laid out in 1898 on a portion of the leased property, and a few homes on that street today date from that period. Charles Morse died in 1900, but the seed business continued under the name Ferry Morse in San Francisco and later in Mountain View.

Heavy immigration from Italy, the Azores and Portugal began in the 1890s. Many immigrants had been agricultural workers in their homeland and some became tenant farmers and worked in the canneries on a seasonal basis. Most lived with relatives who had arrived earlier and had already purchased property. Eventually many were able to buy land for themselves, although they had to supplement their income with cannery work. Italians and Portuguese, therefore, were not long-term sources of cheap labor for the orchardists, as the Chinese had been.

By 1900 there were several Japanese men living in the area of today's Sunnyvale. They were accepted only to fill the labor gap left by the decreasing number of Chinese. As was the case with the Chinese, there were almost no women. Interestingly enough, however, many Japanese men identified themselves as married, some for as long as thirty or forty years. Presumably their wives, who did not live in Santa Clara County, remained in Japan or Hawaii when the men came to California in search of work all those years before.[38]

Even though the Japanese could not own land, they did not remain a source of cheap labor for very long, but became competitors in the market. They began to form permanent communities because women began to arrive as "picture brides" after the turn of the century, and families formed. The movement from migratory labor to farm tenancy for the Japanese was the combined result of the establishment of families, group resistance to labor exploitation, and the formation of partnerships and collectives.[39] Japanese farmers became increasingly independent when

they sold their surplus crops directly to San Francisco, Sacramento, or Oakland markets via bay transportation from Alviso. In 1908 the Japanese tenant farmers at Agnew formed the Japanese Agricultural Alliance to establish social and economic solidarity among the Japanese of the valley.[40] Other farmers resented the independence of the Japanese because it deprived them of a cheap source of labor.[41]

In the mid 1890s, a German couple, Rudolph and Charlotta Muender bought twelve acres at Evelyn and Pastoria avenues and planted prunes, cherries, and peaches. Rudolph is credited with building the Sunnyvale Water Works and contributing to the construction of the Encina School.[42] The two also became merchants in town, building the Muender hotel.

A Portuguese immigrant, Antone Vargas, also personified the changes that occurred in land ownership on the former Bay View land and throughout the valley. He was a farm laborer on the Martin Murphy, Jr. land that was to become Sunnyvale. Early in the 1890s, managing Murphy heir, Bernard Murphy, stipulated that Vargas could continue farming wheat in return for 25% of the crop. Vargas hauled his harvest to Jagle's Landing, near present-day Moffett Field, for water shipment to San Francisco because he could not afford the rail shipping rates. When much of the Murphy estate succumbed to the depression in the 1890s and was divided and sold, Murphy heirs sold two hundred acres to realtor Walter Crossman for $38,000. Antone Vargas and his new wife Mary, purchased ten acres from Crossman and built a house for their large family on Mary Avenue. In 1900, one of their twelve children, Manuel, planted two redwood saplings he had brought home from an outing to Pescadero, on either side of the entryway to the Vargas farm. Towering over Mary Avenue today, the trees have been designated local heritage landmarks. After the turn of the century, Antone Vargas decided to get out of wheat farming and he planted apricot trees to supply local canneries. He supplemented his seasonal income by hauling gravel for the county's road-paving projects.[43]

Nurseryman Frank Chapman Willson had bought a

Frank Chapman Willson standing near one of his experimental walnut trees. Willson retired from the general nursery business to concentrate his efforts on his orchards. Courtesy Sunnyvale Historical Society & Museum Association.

small piece of property near today's El Camino and Pastoria Avenue in 1894 and in 1898 he added a larger parcel of land and built a home. According to Chapman's son Harold, this property was the first piece of the Murphy ranch that was sold. Willson operated his "Encinal Nursery," experimented with hybridization of various strains of walnuts and produced "Willson's Wonder Walnuts." By 1912, Willson went out of the nursery business and concentrated his efforts on his orchards.[44] The oversized Willson walnuts gained notoriety in gourmet shops across the country, and for a few years, the prestigious department store Neiman Marcus bought the giant walnut shells and actually used them as unique packaging for expensive ladies' gloves. Willson's efforts were carried on by his son who continued to farm the land until the 1950s.

The collection of small orchardists of diverse ethnic origin, farm laborers, cannery workers and managers, and local merchants combined to form the emerging town clustered near "Murphy Station," completing the dramatic transition from a highly lucrative wheat and cattle ranch to hundreds of immigrant family-owned, commercial farms. The community was ripe for consolidation, which caught the attention of San José real estate developer Walter Crossman as he planned his "City of Destiny."

Chapter 2

"CITY OF DESTINY"

Walter Everett Crossman,[1] a Wisconsin-born businessman, settled with his wife Diana Angel and their two children Walter and Pauline in San José in the late 1880s. Taking notice of the upheaval in land ownership in the Santa Clara Valley, Crossman embarked on a real estate career. In many respects, the fedora-wearing, cigar-smoking Crossman was a "wheeler-dealer" and opportunist. Not only did he act as real estate agent, but he also was buyer and seller, lender and borrower, notary public, front-man for other purchasers, and later, president of the chamber of commerce. He saw an opportunity to buy land cheap from Murphy heirs who were busy with their own lives and careers and who displayed little interest in expending the time and money to maintain the 4,800 acres that was theirs collectively.

In 1897 Crossman purchased two hundred acres which today is the land directly adjacent to the railstop. He laid out streets, had the land surveyed to offer standard sized one-acre lots for sale and called the new town "Murphy." Advertisements proclaimed "Beautiful Murphy" and the San Jose Mercury printed a layout of the emerging village. In the following several years, he bought more land in his own name and later formed a joint stock corporation, the Sunnyvale Land Company.

In 1897 Fred Cornell opened a general store near the rail depot at the corner of Murphy (at that time called "Main Street") and Evelyn avenues. Stocking everything from farm tools to hair ribbon, Cornell's mercantile also served as the local post office. Postal boxes in the store bore the names of Barney Murphy and some who had already settled nearby like Rudolph Muender, Henry Martens, T. Spencer and Alphonso Schurra, while others receiving mail at Cornell's, found their letters in the general delivery box. The postal station was called *Encinal* (literally, where the live oak grows), probably so named by the locals. Crossman's attempt to rename the area "Murphy" had not had the impact he had hoped. In addition, Cornell, postmaster as well as general merchant, was informed by the United States Postal Department that other towns in California had already taken names very similar to "Encinal" and "Murphy," therefore another name would need to be chosen for the postal stop. Local residents and town promoters somehow reached a consensus and named the town "Sunny-vale," and the post office was officially so christened on January 7, 1901.[2] Walter Crossman was overjoyed with the name, for it served very well to entice citizens from foggy San Francisco to venture to Santa Clara County to view his development.

One of his early sales was to Alphonse and Mary Ann Schurra, French immigrants who bought land in 1898. Their daughter Elsie recalled, "The house was built in 1899 and my father made it a real showplace, he was very classy. Everything was painted white: the carriage room, the barn for the horses and the cow."[3] The Schurras raised their three children in the town, and within a decade, their son Albert opened his candy store on the 100 block of Murphy Avenue,

Post card of Encina School built in 1897, the first grammar school in Sunnyvale. Courtesy Sunnyvale Historical Society & Museum Association.

a delight to all the townspeople.

In February of 1899, some of the same local businessmen formed the Encina School District and collected $4,000 to build Encina School near the south end of today's Sunnyvale Town Center Mall. It opened in September of that year and for the first time, local children did not have to venture to Mountain View for school. The local schoolhouse became a selling point for the infant community.

Crossman carefully strategized his marketing plan to draw potential buyers and investors to Sunnyvale by inviting manufacturers to open shop in the town, thereby offering jobs to hundreds of people. He envisioned his factory town as an ideal community with a perfect balance between industry and agriculture. He dubbed the town the "City of Destiny," invoking the notion that the success of Sunnyvale was preordained and simply needed to be lived out by those with enough foresight to settle there. He advertised his recently acquired property in the national weekly, Colliers magazine, identifying Sunnyvale as part of "poor man's paradise" where hard work produced a plentiful bounty.[4] Crossman also ran ads in Bay Area newspapers, and invited potential buyers for a free train ride

to Sunnyvale and a picnic barbecue awaiting their arrival. Hannah and Carl Olson, Swedish immigrants living in San Francisco, responded to the advertisement and took the train to view the single-acre lots available for $150 to $200. They purchased five acres on McKinley Avenue, between Taaffe and Murphy avenues, later buying a large orchard where family descendants owned and operated the last remaining cherry orchard in Sunnyvale, a short distance from the original property on McKinley.[5]

When potential buyers like the Olsons stepped from the train, they saw a tiny hamlet clustered near the rail stop, which was a sharp contrast to the crowded, bustling city of San Francisco. The air was fresh and clean, fruit orchards were visible in all directions, and the sun shone warmly. Crossman would have greeted them, ushered them to his buggy, and chauffeured them down Murphy Avenue, past Cornell's store, the blacksmith's shop, and over toward the new school. If language was a barrier between the salesman and client, they worked it out with gesture and visual communication. The thought of owning their own piece of land, unthinkable in the city, was enough incentive for many immigrant families to do business with Crossman in his new town. The buyers most often hired their own carpenters to build their homes, and Norwegian Brynel Brynelson who had built his own home on Washington Street, offered his services as carpenter and plumber to many newcomers.[6]

The Trubschenck family, Danish immigrants, moved to Sunnyvale from San Francisco just after the turn of the century as well. Herman Nicolai Trubschenck opened the Pioneer Drug Store on Murphy Avenue while his wife Caroline became one of the first insurance agents in town. They built their home on a lot purchased from Crossman at Taaffe and Washington streets where they raised their four children Ruby, Harvey, William and Ida. The children attended Mountain View High School, and the family was very involved in the local community.

Crossman needed more cash to buy additional property to carry out his objective to develop the "factory town," so he formed the Sunnyvale Land Company to

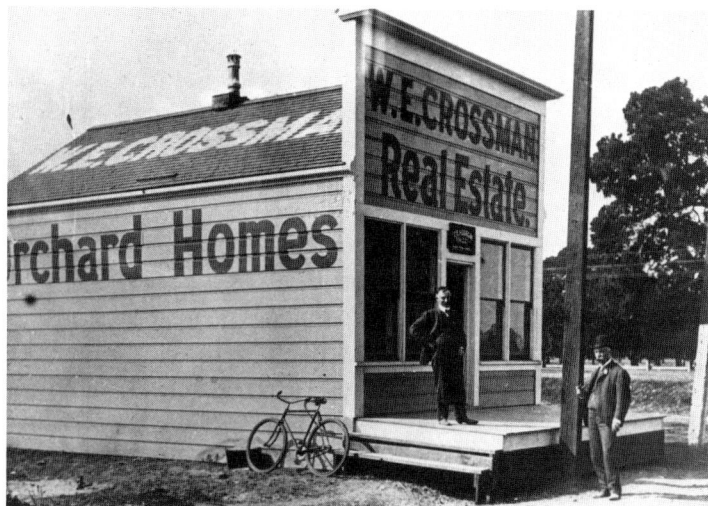

Walter Crossman (right) outside his real estate office with railroad tracks in background in Sunnyvale. Crossman often got around the emerging town on his bicycle. Courtesy Sunnyvale Historical Society & Museum Association.

encourage more investors in his "City of Destiny." He purchased other pieces of property, and continued to sell to immigrants, farmers and some businesses. Walter was the president of the corporation, and his wife Diana served as secretary. Both had signing privileges and their signatures appear on numerous deeds.[7] Crossman's son, Walter A., followed in his father's footsteps and also became a realtor for a time after graduating from Stanford University.

Slowly but surely new businesses appeared in Sunnyvale, with brand new structures cropping up near Murphy Avenue and the rail depot. A dried fruit packing business bought property from the Land Company just east of the rail station in 1904. It was subsequently bought out and called Madison and Bonner Dried Fruit Packers, beginning a long tradition of dried fruit production in Sunnyvale. They dried fruit produced by local farmers, packed it and shipped it directly from their plant by rail to Eastern markets via San Francisco. The Madison and Bonner building, later known as the Del Monte building, was a seed germinating and distribution center for many years for California Pack-

ing Corporation, (Del Monte). It was named a heritage landmark by the City of Sunnyvale, rescued from the wrecking ball, and in 1993 moved across the street to city-owned property.

The Jubilee Incubator Company, a poultry farm supply firm specializing in brooders and incubators, relocated from Oakland and built a facility just east of the Madison and Bonner plant, also along the railroad. Jubilee became synonymous with incubators, and as the story goes, their name on an incubator was "much like 'Sterling' on silver." Jubilee's owners expected the market for their products to expand in the Sunnyvale area because of the availability of farm land.

Goldy Machine Company began to build a machine shop in 1905, but suffered a setback in the earthquake the following year, and their opening was delayed until 1907. The San Francisco earthquake of April 18, 1906 was felt quite dramatically in Sunnyvale, and it proved to be a major economic turning point for the town. Although damage was not nearly as extensive as in more heavily populated areas of the Santa Clara Valley, the San Jose Mercury reported that Sunnyvale's "principal damage was to the Goldy Machine Works. Its great smokestack lies in ruins and the buildings were badly shaken up."[8] Newspaper photos of Goldy showed the huge brick chimney collapsed in a heap and a portion of the roof caved-in.

For Mr. Crossman, however, the initial shock of the earthquake was shortlived and he did not miss a beat in his campaign for a factory town. Just four days after the earthquake, he took out a half-page ad in the San Jose Mercury:

Sunnyvale has gone through the late catastrophe in better shape than any town in Santa Clara county; therefore feel assured that the future for us is absolutely assured. Citizens of San Francisco will be coming our way for their homes and places of business. Already we have located a number of families from the stricken city. All of the cities and towns affected will be soon built; but Sunnyvale, being so situated that it was less

21

affected, will reap a greater benefit, as new manufacturing plants and business houses will spring up immediately. Now is the time to be strong hearted, for the future of Sunnyvale is absolutely assured. Remember that opportunity has no place of [sic] knockers and that now is the time for every citizen to do his best. Yours for Sunnyvale, W. E. Crossman, President, Sunnyvale Land Company.[9]

Perhaps Crossman was seeking more to reassure himself and his stockholders of Sunnyvale's future economic viability than to console local townspeople.

Crossman seized the opportunity to promote industrial growth in Sunnyvale by offering free land to companies that would relocate or build new facilities in Sunnyvale. He predicted correctly that new businesses would find this incentive hard to resist. The post-earthquake boom was fodder for his "City of Destiny," and promotion of his land holdings continued enthusiastically.

At the end of 1906, Sunnyvale Land Company deeded thirty-two acres adjacent to the Southern Pacific rail line to Joshua Hendy Iron Works, a victim of the San Francisco earthquake. The firm's founder, Joshua Hendy, had been a gold rush immigrant and a highly successful nineteenth-century industrialist. He had established a machine shop to produce mining equipment in San Francisco in 1856, where he invented a hydraulic gravel elevator and the Hydraulic Giant Monitor which virtually replaced placer mining. The business thrived, expanding to three buildings before Hendy's death in 1891. Nephews Samuel and John Hendy took over manufacturing operations, which included producing a high-pressure water nozzle, similar to the Giant Monitor, which was used in dam construction and in building the Panama Canal. Public works fixtures such as water plugs and China Town's lamp standards were among other Hendy products.

All three San Francisco buildings of the Hendy Iron Works were destroyed by fire in the 1906 earthquake and Samuel Hendy lost his life. John Hendy responded to Walter

Crossman's invitation to earthquake victims and relocated his manufacturing business to Sunnyvale. Hendy's mother-in-law lived in nearby San José, which was another reason he agreed to move south.[10] The sales and contracts office of Joshua Hendy Iron Works, however, remained in San Francisco.

The Sunnyvale plant was operational by the end of 1907. The main building, a machine shop and assembly room, was an eighth of a mile long, but even that could not accommodate some of the more sizable products. Some mining equipment and engine components had to be assembled outside. The foundry was almost 50,000 square feet and was the largest on the West Coast for many years.[11]

Libby, McNeill & Libby also began construction on a fruit cannery about three-quarters of a mile west of the rail station in 1906 just after the earthquake. Libby was a meat-packing company based in Chicago, and had recently expanded its products to include canned milk. The Sunnyvale plant was Libby's first venture into canned fruits and vegetables. The free land near the railstop offered easy access to fruit and a potentially large labor force. It did not take long for Libby, McNeill & Libby to become the largest employer in Sunnyvale.

From the very beginning, Santa Clara Valley cannery workers were predominantly women. As early as the 1870s

Post card of the yard of Hendy Iron Works, early twentieth century. Courtesy Sunnyvale Historical Society & Museum Association.

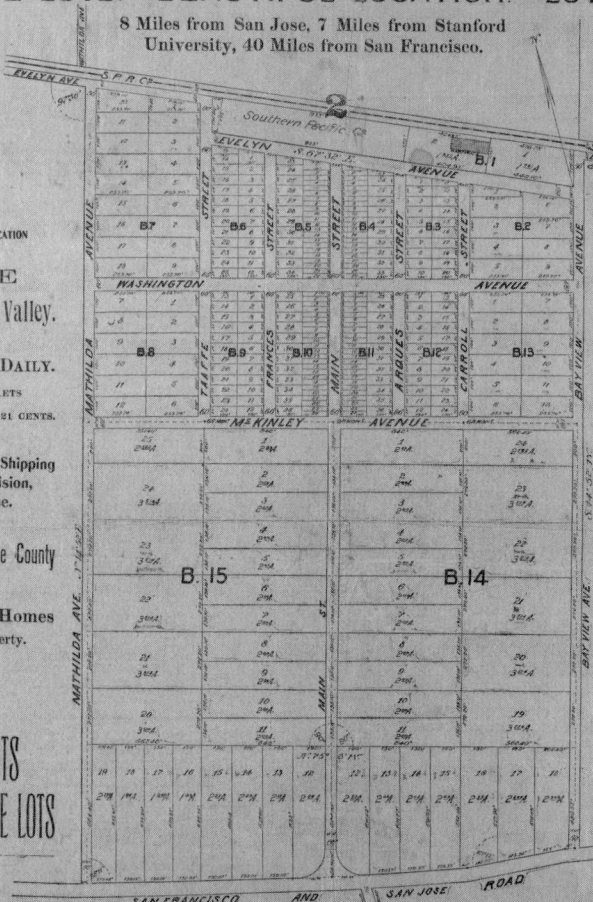

Advertisement in San Jose Daily Mercury depicting a map filed with the county surveyor by Walter Crossman of "Beautiful Murphy," July 4, 1897. Courtesy San Jose Mercury News and Sunnyvale Historical Society & Museum Association.

canneries were actively recruiting women, and by 1900, 70% of the county cannery labor force was female. The seasonal work was so intensive that it disrupted traditional domestic roles. The Sunnyvale Standard reflected the local attitude when a male reporter observed that "work at the cannery occupies the time of a large percent of the female population of the town. Result—many a man has to do the cooking!"[12] Employed women were an accepted economic necessity for Sunnyvale families.

Sunnyvale Canneries, east of the center of town, also built and opened in 1907. George Hooke, hired as president, had been the director of the Los Gatos Canneries. In a typical season, Sunnyvale Canneries employed four hundred people and shipped tons of fresh cherries to be turned into maraschinos.[13]

Commercial development was accompanied by sales of farm land in the wake of the earthquake. At the end of May 1906, Henry and Josephine Stelling bought the former Briggs house and a little over fifty acres of land. They set about remodeling the farmhouse, which had suffered a fire a few years earlier, and added cherry trees to the apricots and prunes planted by Briggs.

The arrival of the telephone caused great excitement in the tiny town when the first switchboard was installed in August of 1906 in the back of Cecil Stubbs' Stationery Store on Murphy Avenue. The original paying customers were George W. James, Charles Parkinson, Bernard Murphy, Goldy Machine Company, Walter Crossman, and Fred Cornell, all active in business in the community. Very shortly thereafter, the list grew to twenty-five subscribers. Telephone service operated out of various buildings under the direction of Cecil Stubbs until 1934 when Pacific Bell took over.[14]

True to form, in addition to his many functions as developer, real estate agent, promoter and notary, Crossman formed and headed a local chamber of commerce at the end of 1906. He published a promotional pamphlet through the Black Cat Press which also put out the town's newspaper the Sunnyvale Standard. Entitled "Sunnyvale: 'The City of

Destiny,'" it underscored appealing attributes:

> To those who are contemplating a change from their present station in life, be it from the disagreeable city, or farm, to a country gifted by God with all the endowments of natural beauty, climate, and richness of soil, developed by human energy and progress to a commercial center of thriving manufactories, and mercantile success, to those, we present these facts, based upon actual conditions, and given with a feeling, that whoever may be so fortunate as to personally investigate them, will find the conditions far above what they anticipate, so that in every statement we make herein your decision can only be "We have made good."[15]

Reports in the development section of Sunset Magazine were reiterated in Crossman's pamphlet, and indicated that for the year 1907, $430,000 was expended for improvements by factories. Houses accounted for expenditures of $150,000, while $275,000 was spent for building lots. Total expenditures in Sunnyvale for 1907 were $996,700, indicating an active, growing community.[16] Post-earthquake land prices were touted as $200 per acre in five-to-ten acre plots within

Sunnyvale's bank building. Courtesy Sunnyvale Historical Society & Museum Association.

two miles of the rail depot. Outlying areas could be had for less, while smaller one acre lots were still available within walking distance of Murphy Avenue, Libby's and the Iron Works.

In December 1905, Iowa native Charles Clifton Spalding, an investor in the Sunnyvale Land Company, organized the Bank of Sunnyvale with a starting capital of $25,000 and in 1907 he built a red brick building at 197 S. Murphy Avenue to house the bank. In addition to serving as bank president, Spalding was elected to the California legislature, and subsequently elected county coroner. Spalding's wife Emma died in 1910 and the following year he married Jessie Parkman. She was influential in her own right later in life when she took over her husband's term as county coroner. Together they were prominent Sunnyvale citizens for their entire lives. Charles remained on as bank manager after the bank was sold to the Bank of Italy in 1922 and was town treasurer for many years.

Apricot drying at the Stowell family property early 1900s. Courtesy Dolly Stowell to City of Sunnyvale. Inset: *Stowell family farm house on today's Saratoga-Sunnyvale Road, circa 1900. Courtesy Sunnyvale Historical Society & Museum Association.*

Spalding's sister Minnie, married Charles L. Stowell a native of the same Iowa town as the Spaldings, which aligned the two families in various real estate deals and business ventures. The brothers-in-law built the Stowell-Spalding building at 198 S. Murphy, whose second story was truly multi-purpose and served as the first public meeting hall for the town, the Grange hall, and a Baptist place of worship, among many others. Spalding and Stowell are credited with building most of the commercial buildings on the 100 block of Murphy Avenue in the first decade of the town's life as well as the 1917 Sunnyvale Post Office on Washington Street.

The Spalding family initially lived at 759 Sunnyvale-Saratoga Road, in a turn-of-the-century home built by Charles' father John Spalding. They also owned and operated 250 acres along El Camino Real of cherry, apricot, prune, and peach orchards with Charles' brother Clyde Spalding and Clyde's brother-in-law F. D. Calkins. In the 1920s, the Spaldings had a new home designed by architect William Weeks, and they built it on fashionable North Sunnyvale Avenue.

The Stowells bought twenty-five acres on Highway 9 or the Saratoga-Sunnyvale Road in 1920. As years passed, the Stowells added to their land and bought other properties as well. Charles Stowell eventually became president of the Sunnyvale Land Company, succeeding Walter Crossman.

Tempted by all the development, two lumber companies and a paint manufacturer opened for business in Sunnyvale. Over twenty builder-carpenters came to town and built hundreds of new houses. The population grew and the little town had 1,268 residents by 1908, 271 of whom were children. Since its turn-of-the-century beginning, the budding town boasted a weekly newspaper, the Sunnyvale Standard, a bank, a volunteer fire department, growing local industries, and churches of various denominations. St. Martin's Catholic Church was built in 1910 at McKinley and Sunnyvale avenues. In addition to the Sunnyvale Land Company, Walter Crossman operated Sunnyvale Guarantee Loan and Investment Company out of his Murphy Avenue

office. Several other businesses sprouted on the as yet unpaved main street including C. D. Samuels' Columbia Cyclery, L. H. Vishoot's Sunnyvale Hardware, and competition for Mr. Crossman in the Sim brothers' Sunnyvale Investment Company. A short distance from the main street, were larger companies like Libby's, Hendy, Jubilee Incubator and Goldy Machine Company. Walter Crossman's dream of a factory town seemed about to become a reality.

In 1909, the Santa Clara County Board of Supervisors granted the status of a separate township for Sunnyvale, which allowed the town to hire its own law enforcement officer. The community continued to rely on local volunteers for fire protection. The wood-planked sidewalks and frame buildings were a constant concern, and most men within running distance were part of the volunteer corp.

The "destiny" refrain, so obvious in the first years of Sunnyvale, played again and again in chamber of commerce literature promoting the glories of the town. The lyrics of a 1910 song entitled "Sunnyvale" reflect the sense of optimism of the little community:

Sun-ny-vale 'tis of thee,
    City of Destiny,
Of thee we sing;
    Home of the Iron Works
Place where nobody shirks —
    But helps to boost along,
Sweet Sunnyvale!

Vale of the genial clime,
    Good weather all the time,
To thee we sing;
    With cold we're undistressed,
With heat we're not oppressed,
    With enterprise we're blest,
In Sunnyvale!

Come, help us boost our town,

And spread its fair renown
To all the world;
Help us to build it up,
'Till Plenty's bounteous cup,
With good things well filled up,
Shall overflow![17]

Sunnyvale Land Company investors and many local business leaders, including Charles Spalding and Walter Crossman, actively campaigned to incorporate the town of Sunnyvale. Proponents of incorporation said that the town would enjoy greater exposure at the state, county, and regional levels. The plan outlined specific boundaries for the incorporated area, which included a narrow strip of land extending from the town's center to the bay. The chamber of commerce, led by Walter Crossman, claimed that this narrow link with the bay would enable the town to establish "Port Sunnyvale" which was perceived as an incentive to industrialists to locate their businesses in Sunnyvale because it would increase commerce between the town and other ports-of-call on San Francisco Bay.

The opposition, led by S. N. Goldy, vice-president of Goldy Machine Company, claimed incorporation would increase taxes for the townspeople. Other opponents suggested that Sunnyvale, which had no saloons and was a "dry" town, would go "wet" if incorporation were implemented. In reality, the "dry" district boundaries would have remained the same regardless of the outcome of the election. This argument, however, persuaded some residents to vote against incorporation. Ironically, a local temperance group was not convinced by the argument and favored incorporation.

A special election was held in Sunnyvale on December 10, 1912 which resulted in the incorporation of the town on December 24, 1912. Libby's and Hendy Iron Works gave their workers time off work with pay to encourage them to vote in favor of incorporation and presumably Goldy Machine Company did the same for the opposition. There were 248 votes cast in favor of incorporation and 102 op-

posed. California had adopted women's right to vote in 1911, and Sunnyvale's incorporation election was the first ballot ever cast by some local women. Ida Trubschenck was elected city clerk in this first election, initiating a long line of women elected officials in the town's history. Affectionately called "Aunt Ida" by many townspeople, Miss Trubschenck became a renowned and beloved Sunnyvale citizen. She meticulously maintained the financial and public works records and all correspondence of the city for over forty years.[18]

The first mayor was Civil War veteran Harvey R. Fuller who earned one more vote than O. E. Linden. Banker Charles Spalding was elected treasurer and W. B. McNeil became Sunnyvale's first elected marshal.[19] A Standard editorialist was clearly in favor of incorporation:

Tuesday's election has shown to the world that Sunnyvale understood the knock of Opportunity at her door and that she has extended the glad hand of welcome. The count of ballots has proven that full three-fourths of her citizens have red blood in their veins and that they will henceforth move her wheels of progress steadily onward to a glorious destiny.[20]

The vote for incorporation was celebrated in April 1913, when the new town trustees invited residents and officials from all over the county to view the proposed site of "Port Sunnyvale," otherwise known as Jagel's Landing. Newspapers recorded the string of cars wending its way to the port as "the largest automobile parade in Sunnyvale's history."[21] Incorporation and the growth that occurred in the first decade of the twentieth century, without a doubt, set Sunnyvale on course for future industrial development.

There was some criticism of Crossman in Sunnyvale and power struggles ensued between the Spalding-Stowell coalition and Walter Crossman. A 1913 editorial accused Crossman of greatly exaggerating the financial statement of Joshua Hendy Iron Works in order to appease worried Sunnyvale Land Company stockholders: "this land company

[Crossman's] has, not only in this instance, but in times past, issued these false statements. . ."[22] The editorialist was specifically concerned that investors were calculating their return based on unsubstantiated figures.

Although Walter Crossman continually extolled the town, it was never the overwhelming financial success that he had hoped. In 1913, the Land Company sold 180 acres to a Mr. Atkinson in San José who intended to resell the land in five and ten acre increments to new settlers. Conflicts erupted among the majority stockholders in the Land Company when Charles Spalding and Charles L. Stowell thought Crossman had mortgaged too heavily and had too much control over Sunnyvale's economic future. To make matters worse, Crossman was also besieged with family problems. His son and daughter-in-law were estranged from each other, and the younger Crossman was accused of kidnapping his four-year-old son from a crowded San José restaurant. The snatching caused a huge spectacle when young Crossman, a former Stanford athlete, raced from the cafeteria with the little boy in his arms and jumped in his car to speed away. His astonished wife and enraged mother-in-law chased him, screaming wildly, as they jumped on the running boards of his car.[23] Needless to say, the press had a field day, which did nothing for Crossman's local popularity. The family moved to San Francisco in 1913, and operated the Land Company out of offices there until ultimately, the senior Crossman sold his 270,000 shares of the Sunnyvale Land Company's total outstanding stock of 340,000 shares to Stowell and Spalding. Stowell became the manager of the Land Company and immediately called for a stockholders meeting and closed the San Francisco office. The Land Company's Sunnyvale office on Murphy Avenue became the new home and Fred Cornell served as secretary of the corporation. The Sunnyvale Standard noted that "A more liberal policy is to be adopted regarding the sale [of Land Company] land . . . ." The article continued that "valuations will be reduced and wage earners and other people of small means will be given an opportunity to secure home sites on

Post card of Sunnyvale from the north side of the railroad tracks, looking down Murphy Avenue. Note the path on the lower right side which led to the remaining Murphy property. The building near the tracks on the right was the Madison & Bonner Dried Fruit packinghouse, later the Del Monte building which was designated a landmark and moved across Evelyn Avenue in 1993. Courtesy Sunnyvale Historical Society & Museum Association.

the most liberal terms."[24] Crossman retired to Southern California toward the end of 1915, leaving behind his "City of Destiny."

Sunnyvale blossomed into a middle-sized town. In 1913, El Camino Real in Sunnyvale was paved, making the main street in town more accessible. Murphy Avenue, however, was not paved until 1916. Some housing tracts were built just after incorporation, including Diana Park, the Fair Oaks addition and Colonel Fuller's tract.

The first decade of the town's existence put Sunnyvale on a decidedly pro-growth and pro-industrial path. A political structure was set up whereby town trustees managed civic affairs and encouraged economic growth which set the stage for the years of World War I and the 1920s. It became a time of moderate population growth, increased ethnic diversity, modernization in fruit orcharding and canning, as well as a time of a greater presence of seasonal workers and migrant laborers in Sunnyvale.

Chapter 3

A FARMING COMMUNITY

Although Sunnyvale continued to experience moderate population growth after incorporation, it remained primarily a farming community. Crossman's "factory town" did not fully materialize. While buildings went up on Murphy Avenue, agricultural developments in fruit and vine production continued on farms only a short distance away. A new grammar school, financed by a $25,000 school bond, opened in 1917. Sunnyvale Grammar School or McKinley School as it was often referred to, replaced the old Encina School as the hub of the community.

Most Portuguese, Spanish, French or Italian immigrants were able to buy their own farms and plant orchards to join the cycle of production. The Japanese, however, were victims of "yellow peril" hysteria sweeping California in the early part of the twentieth century, and were subject to the Alien Land Laws of 1913 which disallowed land ownership by Asian aliens. The San José Grange, which included Sunnyvale farmers, sponsored a meeting in August of 1913 to develop a plan to advertise Santa Clara County in order to draw "a good class of settlers" to the area. They were quite fearful, however, of "Asiatics and other unassimilable foreigners." The Grangers felt that "it is pretty clear that, as far as farming is concerned, the only people worth while for us to attract here are those able to purchase small tracts of land which can be improved and cultivated by the family help."[1] Their sentiments were transparently anti-Japanese, merely reflecting the intent of the Alien Land Laws. The

restrictions caused an uproar in Japan and in Washington D.C., however, because politicians from both countries were attempting to maintain trade relations. Some Japanese farmers skirted the laws by purchasing land in their American-born child's name or in the name of a fictitious corporation.[2]

Tsunegusu Yonemoto immigrated to Sunnyvale from Japan in 1917 with his wife and fifteen-year-old son. The couple had another son in 1919, and since they were disallowed from owning land, they purchased it in the name of their American baby son. The 1920 census manuscript clearly notes Mr. Yonemoto as a renter, while his ten-month old baby owned the land, free and clear.[3] The family opened the Yonemoto Carnation Nursery which eventually had eight green houses on the North Murphy Avenue property. The Immigration Act of 1924 put an end to additional Japanese immigration and helped to suppress competition posed by already successful Japanese farmers who were independently shipping their own products to San Francisco. By this time, the Japanese had clearly grown beyond their status as migrant laborers and they no longer supplied the needed labor force to harvest other farmers' fruit.

Spaniards filled the labor gap left by the Japanese, and by 1916 a Spanish enclave had emerged in Sunnyvale and Mountain View. A large group of poor families had sailed from Spain in search of work in the sugar cane fields of Hawaii. They were promised grants of land after five years of labor, but the promises proved false. James Gil, the son of one of the Spanish immigrants, recalled his father's disillusionment with Hawaii:

> According to my dad, when the ship arrived in Honolulu, they herded all of the Spaniards to a fumigation plant. They all stripped down and were fumigated with chemicals . . . . Looking back, a lot of the Spaniards were promised that if they stayed five years, they would get an acre of land, plus the house they were living in. I haven't heard to this day of anyone getting the acre promised.[4]

Two dissatisfied men left Hawaii and ended up working in apricot and cherry orchards in Sunnyvale. Word got back to their countrymen in Hawaii of the better working conditions, and almost the entire group of Spaniards transplanted itself to the Sunnyvale-Mountain View area.[5]

Within a few years, many Spanish families formed the *Sociedad Cervantes Española* which was an association to raise funds to support Spanish families in time of crisis or death. Eventually the *Sociedad* became more of a social organization and it sponsored dances and dramatic presentations for the Spanish community. During the 1930s, the *Sociedad* purchased a former hardware store as a new headquarters which was torn down and replaced in the 1950s. At one time, 500 families belonged to *Sociedad Cervantes Española*.

When war in Europe broke out in 1914, Americans were in no mood to participate and they supported President Wilson's intent to remain neutral. The next few years however, drew the United States inextricably toward war, and the impact of American participation was felt directly in Sunnyvale, California. For one thing, the Selective Service Act of 1917 called local boys to the service of their country. In support of their sons, brothers, and husbands, Sunnyvale church and women's groups formed sewing circles to send wool socks, bandages and other supplies overseas.

What made the war even more obvious in Sunnyvale, however, was the increased activity at Hendy Iron Works. New contracts were awarded for naval equipment and weaponry, which increased employment to nine hundred workers, running in shifts round-the-clock. The Iron Works produced eleven state-of-the-art 2,800 horse-power, triple expansion reciprocating steam engines, called "up and downers," for cargo ships which earned an international reputation for the Sunnyvale plant.[6]

Another indication of the war's presence in Sunnyvale came from a more unexpected front. Fruit growers, canners, and packers initially feared that the war would drain the local manpower, thus disabling the fruit industry. What they did not expect, however, was a huge increase in the demand for canned and preserved fruit and vegetables.

Tikvica family members display their homegrown cherries on the Sunnyvale farm, circa 1915. Courtesy City of Sunnyvale.

The troops were in need of nutritious food that would keep for months at a time. These expanding markets fostered the commercialization of fruit orchards in Sunnyvale which in turn demanded greater numbers of cheap seasonal laborers for both the canneries and farms.

The canneries geared up for increased production and urged farmers to produce as large a crop as possible. The farmers argued that they should only produce what they and their families could harvest because the cost of

Two unidentified Sunnyvale farmers and their truck load of prunes, circa 1920s. Courtesy Sunnyvale Historical Society & Museum Association.

labor was so high. They complained that the restrictions against Asian immigration to California, which they had supported a few short years earlier, left them without a labor force and they lobbied for permitting Chinese laborers into the country as farm workers. A Sunnyvale Standard editorial called for "contracts with coolie brokers . . . for three years at a fixed wage rate, and at the end of their term . . . [they should be] returned to their native land." The writer continued that "Japanese laborers could not be managed so easily, and once here they would become colonists and remain" which was completely undesirable.[7]

When the United States entered the war in Europe, a sense of patriotism surged in the country, along with strong anti-communist feelings which manifested itself as a "red scare." Organized labor was viewed as socialist, and therefore a threat and an affront to patriotic Americans. When labor disputes erupted at the canneries in neighboring San José and Santa Clara in July of 1917, and cannery workers

struck with the support of agricultural workers, tons of fruit rotted on the trees and the canneries came to a standstill. County business leaders were convinced that "outside agitators" and radicals were conspiring to destroy their crops so they bypassed Governor William Stephens and demanded federal troops to guard the canneries. The strike did not spread to Sunnyvale, but it did scare the town's canners and growers. They did not want any interference in meeting increased demand for canned fruit during the war. They began to have high hopes that the war would permanently expand the canned fruit market which was being advertised nationally in nutrition education campaigns to encourage the general public to buy canned fruits and vegetables.

All the while, farmers felt pressure from both labor and canners. Farmer's Union Corporation, a growers' cooperative which had been formed in San José in 1874, had some Sunnyvale members and the National Grange had a chapter in Sunnyvale. These cooperatives were designed to help farmers protect themselves against canners, shippers and distributors taking too much of their profit as author Yvonne Jacobson put it, "so that David could have at least a toehold against Goliath."[8] The farmers sought more control over marketing their product. After the strikes in neighboring towns in the summer of 1917, Sunnyvale growers and town officials saw the need for a local growers' cooperative.

The growers in Sunnyvale were soundly criticized for not forming cooperatives sooner. A Standard editorial claimed that the town would enjoy greater stability and be less susceptible to outside influences or agitation if growers banded together to garner more profit for themselves and passed a portion of it on to labor.

Farmers are recognized to be the slowest people on earth to get together for mutual protection . . . ; the higher cost of living for the laborer must be taken into consideration . . . resulting in a better standard of living for all if some benefit is passed on to the laborers.[9]

Farm equipment show on El Camino Real in Sunnyvale, circa 1920. Courtesy California History Center, Stocklmeir Library/Archives, Michelle Ann Jacobson Collection.

The Sunnyvale Chamber of Commerce and the local growers met in December of 1917 and outlined details to establish a packinghouse for the Prune and Apricot Growers' Association (later called Sunsweet) in order to eliminate the "middleman." Outspoken local advocates included banker Charles Spalding, suffragist Mrs. Sophie Durst, and local shopkeeper Mr. L. H. Vishoot.[10]

Local growers' cooperatives, together with the end of the war, soothed the wounds at home inflicted by labor unrest, but only temporarily. Sunnyvale veterans returned home to work the land, and many of Hendy's wartime employees went back to orchard work. After the war, the Iron Works reduced its work force, but production on crawler tractors, freight car wheel pullers, water wheels and large water contol valves for Hoover Dam, and parts for dredges and diesel engines continued through the 1920s. Although the company employed far fewer workers than during wartime, it remained a viable and well-equipped manufacturing company. John Hendy's death in May of

1920, left an uncertain future for the Iron Works, and the company was eventually sold.

More neighborhoods emerged in Sunnyvale as a result of increased productivity at Hendy and the canneries during the war. In the Bay View and McKinley tract, California bungalows were built and occupied by the town's new workers. The houses had single-car detached garages and front porches under gabled overhangs. The area just south and east of these neighborhoods remained orchards until the 1950s.

A $17,000 bond issue came before the voters in 1919, which proposed creating a park from a nine-acre grove of oak trees, probably the same area where the famous Murphy barbecue was held. Hendy Iron Works contributed $1,000 in support of the park and the chamber of commerce endorsed the project where "on this plot stand some 43 of the best oaks of the grove."[11] The voters, however, did not support the bond issue, and therefore the park was never established. The land was eventually divided and sold and most of the

Giant valve produced by Hendy Iron Works circa 1920. Standing on the left is John Hendy, president of the Iron Works; on the far right is Rex Rexworthy and next to him is Frederick Bennerman who purchased the Iron Works when Hendy died. Courtesy Jesse Brown to the Sunnyvale Historical Society & Museum Association.

oaks were removed.

Still uppermost in the minds of Sunnyvale's business community was the dream of establishing a deep water port on the bay. Even in 1920, activity surrounding the proposed port drew crowds. The South Shore Port Company was established in order to build the long awaited port,

and a board of directors elected officers to launch a fund-raising campaign. Walnut farmer Frank Willson, Charles Stowell, a Mr. King and Mr. Roberts represented Sunnyvale while other directors were from San José, Mountain View, Palo Alto and San Francisco. On a sunny September Sunday in 1920, the company hosted a tour of the former Jagel's Landing, the future "Port Sunnyvale." Like the park, however, and despite numerous efforts, the port never became a reality. Nevertheless, the idea hung around for decades.

Charles Spalding, who had started the Bank of Sunnyvale in the town's early days, decided to sell it to a Palo Alto company in 1919, but he remained on as manager. Within a year, negotiations were underway to sell the bank again, this time to Mr. A. P. Giannini's Bank of Italy. The Sunnyvale branch of the Bank of Italy, managed again by Charles Spalding, was the predecessor of today's local branch of the Bank of America.

By 1920, the population of the incorporated area of Sunnyvale was 1,676, while the combined total of the township including the unincorporated land was 3,390. Even at this early point, it is clear that a relatively small number of people determined town policy since only those within the incorporated area were eligible to vote in town elections. Those living on unincorporated land remained uninvolved in town issues, which ultimately was their downfall in the 1940s and 1950s when their votes to preserve farm land would be critical.

Early in the 1920s, it became obvious that the number of high school students would continue to climb, and a high school was needed in Sunnyvale. William H. Weeks, the architect who designed the Spalding's house, was contracted to draw plans for the new school. During his successful career, Mr. Weeks designed numerous buildings, among them several schools throughout California. In 1925, Fremont High School opened its doors to students for the first time. The building remains today a prime example of Mr. Weeks work, and is a fully functioning and well maintained school.

Sunnyvale's local government officials also knew that they could no longer function out of the old bank building on Murphy Avenue. Plans were drawn for a new city hall which was erected at McKinley and Murphy avenues. The mission style stucco building had a red tile roof and housed municipal court and a library, while its auditorium served as site for numerous social and cultural affairs in Sunnyvale. When construction was complete in 1929, there was no money available for landscaping, so shrubs, cedars and redwoods were donated by local social groups and private citizens.

The post office in Sunnyvale had grown to keep pace with the town since the days of the general delivery box in Fred Cornell's store. By 1917, Sunnyvale had its own post office building on Washington Street, built by Charles Stowell, across from today's Sunnyvale Town Center. Young Joe Stanich, son of Eastern European immigrants, was hired by Postmaster Charles Fuller for odd jobs. His first duty was to raise the flag every morning and stoke the lobby stove fire so patrons would be comfortable when the office opened. Joe became the delivery man when he loaded up the outgoing mail on the horse-drawn buggy to take the mail to catch the morning train. Mail was sorted into two pouches, one "North" and the other "South" and placed in a "catcher pouch" for the appropriate San Francisco or San José-bound train. A "mail crane" stood near the rail tracks, and the catcher pouch hung on the crane so mail car workers on the train could get the mail even on those trains not scheduled to stop in Sunnyvale. When the mail car workers "caught" the pouch, they also "kicked off" another, bound for Sunnyvale. An occasional error in this intricate system sometimes caused crumpled, chewed-up letters, but for the most part, the system was was quite effective.[12] Joe Stanich worked for Sunnyvale's Post Office until long after the horse and buggy were retired, and he witnessed the transition from general delivery to the first town mail carriers, Bill Golick and Willard Peterson who split the town in two and delivered to every house and business.

Sunnyvale had several outspoken and colorful people who played their part in the town's political and social circles. Edwina (Cochrane) Benner was born at Butcher's Corners to Mary and Welford Cochrane in 1885 and was a lifelong influence in Sunnyvale. In 1909, Edwina married Carson Benner, the town's barber, and she worked for many years as office manager at Libby, McNeil & Libby. In 1920, Mrs. Benner was elected to the board of trustees, an early version of the city council, and in 1924 she began her

Joe Stanich hangs mail pouch catcher at Sunnyvale rail station, circa 1920. Courtesy Sunnyvale Historical Society & Museum Association.

term as mayor of Sunnyvale. She is credited with being the first woman mayor in California, and she served a second term as mayor in 1937–1938. She was a continual member of the board of trustees from 1920 to 1945. During World War II, in addition to her many other responsibilities, Mrs. Benner was commissioner of finance and public works in Sunnyvale, chairperson of the local branch of the American Red Cross, and an active member of the chamber of commerce.[13] So popular was Edwina Benner that in the 1950s, the school district named an elementary school in her honor: Edwina Benner School. When Mrs. Benner died in 1955, Mayor Ernest Stout ordered the city hall flags be flown at half mast in her memory.

Mrs. Sophia Durst was also a prominent woman in Sunnyvale and the Bay Area. She was a writer and served for a time as president of the Pacific Coast Woman's Press Association and was a member of the League of American Pen Women. She had been a ardent supporter of women's suffrage and worked closely with Susan B. Anthony when she came to California to campaign for women's right to vote. Durst also formed a close association with Elizabeth Lowe Watson, a Cupertino suffragist and woman preacher.[14] Mrs. Durst organized the Sunnyvale Woman's Study Club which was a social and educational philanthropic club. She authored a book of poetry called Mosaics, and in it a few poems are written specifically about Santa Clara Valley.[15]

Sunnyvale's families depended on physicians in neighboring towns for medical care until the 1920s when a

Sophia Durst, Sunnyvale suffragist, philanthropist and journalist. Photo from Mosaics, copy in Sunnyvale Public Library.

few doctors opened local practices. Doctor Tolbert Watson came from Minnesota and opened an office upstairs in the S-S Building at the corner of Murphy and Washington streets. In 1935, young Doctor Howard Diesner joined Watson's practice, and later married Watson's daughter. Diesner served on Fremont Union High School District's Board from 1939 when Charles Spalding urged him to run for the position, until 1969. In 1956, the Fremont High School Board voted to name the athletic field at Fremont High in honor of Howard Diesner. The doctor also served on the Board of Trustees for the Foothill-De Anza Community College District for many years. Another longtime Sunnyvale physician, Doctor George Armanini, also worked closely with Doctors Watson and Diesner and the three formed the Sunnyvale Medical Clinic in 1946. Doctor George Hall maintained a part-time practice in San José while serving Sunnyvale as well. His Murphy Avenue office was across the street from Watson and Diesner, and his practice was associated with San Jose Hospital.

Many southern and eastern European immigrants to Sunnyvale maintained their ties with families from the "old country." Luka and Kate (Grcich) Pavlina met in Sunnyvale, although their families had originated in what we have known as Yugoslavia. Luka (later anglicized to Louis) was from a small town outside Dubrovnik on the Adriatic coast, while Kate was from the village of Majhovi. They married in 1922 and struggled financially until they were able to purchase five acres of orchard for $8,000 at El Camino Real and Mary Avenue. For a few years, they worked the land themselves, bought additional acreage in the Spalding Tract, and even made their own wine. They socialized with other Eastern European immigrants including the Vidovich and Sevely families. By the 1930s, the Pavlinas needed more help than their family and friends could provide, so like many other farming families, they hired migrant "Okies" and Mexicans to help harvest their annual fruit crop.[16] After World War II, the Pavlinas packed and shipped their cherries, "Pavlina Beautys," to Eastern markets.

Sam and Nina (D'Amico) Monforte bought forty

Sam and Nina Monforte in their orchard near Mary and Evelyn avenues, circa 1940s. Courtesy Ed Fassett, S.J.

Seijo's Bakery opened in 1929, and John and Augustina Seijo provided baked goods for Murphy Avenue patrons. Schurra's Candy Store maintained a faithful patronage, and a few years later, folks would shop at Gimenez Grocers and have their car serviced at Raines Garage. At about this same time, August Lewis founded his Sunnyvale Garbage Company which later became Specialty Garbage. Mr. Lewis' son Harry recalled that garbage collecting was not a very desirable way to make a living when he noted "if you wanted to get a date with a girl, you had to go out of town."[18]

Rose Zamar, a young Lebanese woman, came to Sunnyvale in 1929 even though she did not have legal immigration status. Initially she lived with her sister and brother-in-law, Caramie and John Sayig. She worked picking cherries for Ruel Charles Olson, an orchardist and son of one of Sunnyvale's earliest couples, Charles and Hannah Olson. Rose married the young Olson and they raised their children to grow up loving the trees and a

acres of land at Evelyn and Mary avenues just after they were married in 1926. Sam, an immigrant from Sicily, had earned money as a bricklayer in San Francisco after the earthquake. For the first several years, the couple could not afford to hire any help and they worked the land themselves, primarily growing prunes. Nina, a seamstress by trade, told her grandchildren that she went overnight from wearing white kid gloves and four-inch French heels while making clothes for the wealthy ladies of Stockton, to driving a tractor in Sunnyvale![17] The Monfortes raised their daughter Marianna, who attended local schools, and was the organist at St. Martin's Church.

Mike and Frieda Kirkish opened a clothing store on Murphy Avenue in 1924. A farmer could buy a pair of overalls for $1.25 and take home a dress for his wife for under $4.00. Across the street, Billy Wetterstrom's Barber Shop opened about 1925. The shop's back room had a bathtub that was very busy late on Saturday afternoons when men would buy a shave and a bath before dances at Stowell Hall or a movie at Schurra's Sunnyvale Theatre.

Sunnyvale Creamery and local soda fountain at 200 Murphy Avenue. A corner of the store was set up as a lending library, the first in Sunnyvale, established by the Women's Christian Temperance Union (WCTU), circa 1931. Courtesy Sunnyvale Historical Society & Museum Association, Winters' Family Collection.

Otis Raines greets customers at his Murphy Avenue garage, circa 1920s. Mr. Raines served as mayor of Sunnyvale in the mid-1940s. Courtesy California History Center, Stocklmeir Library/Archives.

Main office of Schuckl Cannery until 1942 when it was moved to its present site on McKinley Avenue. Circa 1930. Courtesy Sunnyvale Historical Society & Museum Association.

farmer's way of life. Rose sold cherries from the Olson Cherry Stand on El Camino Real from the 1930s until well into the 1980s. Her presence became synonymous with cherry season for generations of Santa Clara County cherry lovers, a tradition carried on by her children and grandchildren.

Fruit canning ventures continued to evolve throughout the 1920s. Sunnyvale Canneries, a leader in the local fruit business since the 1906 earthquake, was purchased in 1925 by Schuckl Cannery of Niles, California. Schuckl's was a smaller operation than Libby's, but the plant had its own box factory, blacksmith and carpenter's shop, as well as a syrup room. The company took great pride in its treatment of employees, and was first to provide on-site day care for children of its workers, complete with a playground. By 1930, the company had added a 30,000 square foot warehouse, a label room with a capacity for 18 million labels, and a cooling plant of about 10,000 square feet. They built forty-five cottages to accommodate transient workers.

The seasonal nature of farm and cannery work resulted in both social and economic instability for Sunny-

vale. Santa Clara Valley produced 90% of California's total fruit and vegetable output. In 1930, Sunnyvale's population was 3,094, five of whom were Black and eighty-eight Asian. Half of the total population had foreign-born parents, while 25% were foreign-born themselves.[19] The summer population, however, jumped as high as 6,500 when seasonal fruit pickers and cannery workers came to town. This population fluctuation caused two problems for Sunnyvale which were faced by many other agricultural communities dependent on a seasonal labor force. First, if the population did not jump in the summer, who would harvest, dry or can the fruit? Second, if laborers did come for the summer, where would they live? Sunnyvale Canneries and Libby's supplied some housing on their property, building cabins and cottages for their seasonal workers, but migrant farm workers in Sunnyvale were generally not provided with housing and very often camped in tents or wherever they could find shelter in the orchards.

Author Rudy Calles recalled his Mexican family's annual trek from Southern California to the Santa Clara Valley, or "Prune Heaven" as they called it.

After our arrival, we all pitched in to help establish our residence, which consisted of the one tent that was to be our home for the next three months. Four adults and five children made up our family group of the elite society of pickers of the "King Prune." . . . the work was a combination of pure misery, dirt, painful backs, aching knees, sunburned hands and necks, plus the dismay of knowing that your earnings for all of this 'happiness' would amount to between 80 cents and $1.25 for a ten hour day.[20]

The ever-present search for cheap migrant labor was solved for a time when Filipinos first arrived in Sunnyvale in 1923 and began working in the orchards. They were almost exclusively young, single men and were paid lower wages than any other immigrant group. California agriculturalists had learned that the Japanese had gained much of their economic independence and stability because they established families when picture brides came from Japan. Laws against interracial marriage applied to Filipinos as well as the Chinese and Japanese until the passage of the War Brides Act after the Second World War, and land ownership restrictions kept Sunnyvale Filipinos from buying property. Both sets of laws kept Filipinos at the lowest possible social and economic status and ensured that farmers had a ready supply of farm workers. Growers preferred that Filipinos return to the Philippines when their economic usefulness expired each season, but the Philippine Islands were a United States territory, making Filipinos U. S. Nationals. Thus they had a legal status that protected them from deportation, if not discrimination.

In the summer of 1930, feeling that they were losing work to Filipinos, white farm workers threatened Sunnyvale growers: "Let go your Filipino help, or we'll burn you out." They made good on their threat, and a fire set at the Gallimore ranch in August burned several workers' cabins. Nineteen-year-old Joaquin Somera was killed in the fire, but the county coroner ruled that the victim was "probably accidentally burned." The scare tactics were evidently successful because two contracts for 120 farm workers were cancelled that summer and two hundred Filipino workers at canneries were let go.[21]

Libby's had limited the workday to eight hours in 1922 for employees under age eighteen. Adults had a ten-hour workday, and except for those who worked on the sorting belt, were paid a piece rate. Employees who failed to meet the piecework quota were sent home, which was particularly difficult for older workers. Younger workers preferred the piece-rate system because they would be paid more for harder work. However, the higher wage for more work was a double-edged sword because faster work set new speed standards, causing more pressure for the workers.[22]

Workers were never hired for a season but were hired for a particular fruit. This system "kept you a debtor," as former cannery worker Elizabeth Nicholas recalled. There was no permanence or job security and the worker could not make any complaints if she wanted to be hired for the next fruit. There was simply no other work to be had, particu-

A non-striking apricot grower's fruit dumped on Homestead Road in 1939. He had agreed to accept the canners' price of $30 per ton, but the strikers were holding out for $42.50. Courtesy Sourisseau Academy for State and Local History.

larly for women and older people who were not hired at Hendy Iron Works.[23] Until the formation of a union in 1937, workers were either hired for the duration of a "pack" or had to line up every morning to hear if they would work that day.[24]

According to Elizabeth Nicholas, a union organizer and worker at Libby's, management gave "imported" workers from the San Joaquin Valley priority in employment because they lived on site during the season.[25] Nicholas, an avowed communist, tried to organize the cannery workers and establish a charter with the AFL. Organizing committees were formed at twenty-eight valley canneries, but Nicholas was fired because of her political affiliation and

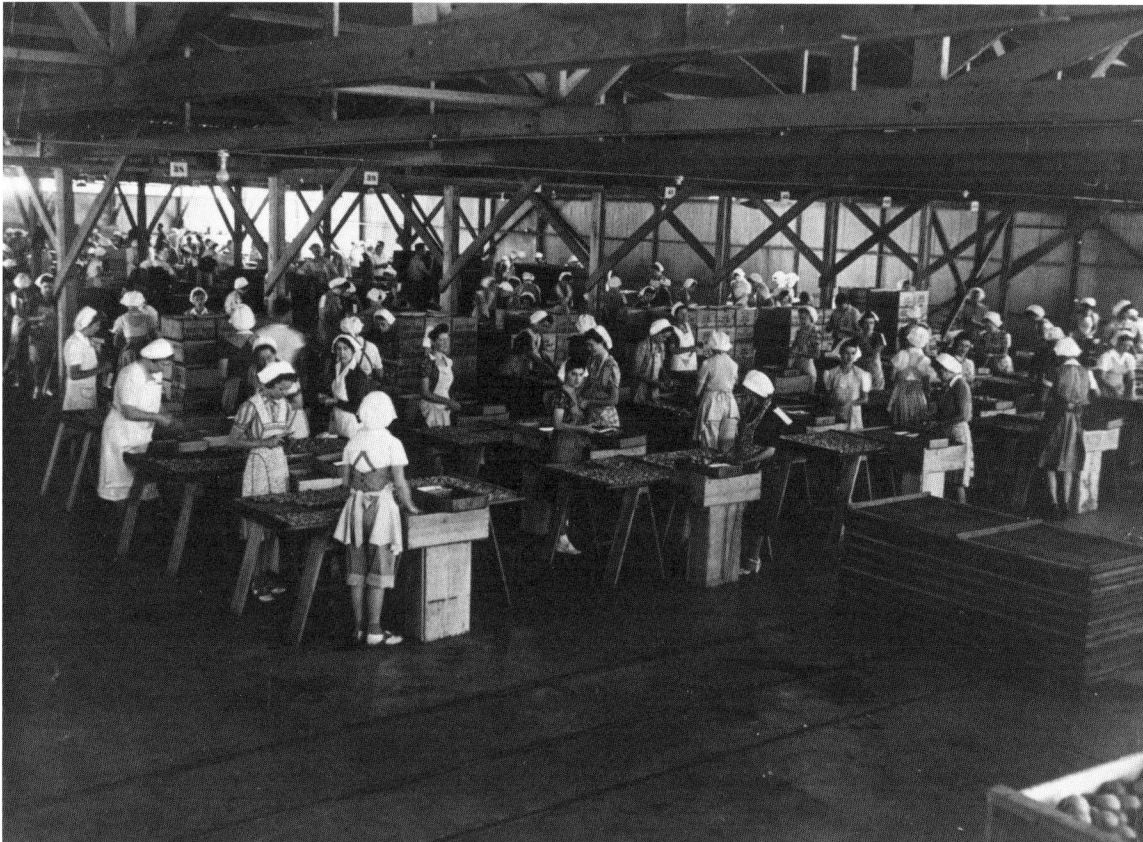

UPPER LEFT:
A cabin at Libby's Cannery where some seasonal cannery workers lived, circa 1930s. Courtesy Sunnyvale Historical Society & Museum Association.

LEFT:
Apricot cutting by women workers, circa 1940s. Courtesy California History Center, Stocklmeir Library/ Archives, Michelle Ann Jacobson Collection.

View of 200 block of Murphy Avenue looking north, circa 1920s. Note Bank of Italy and Wanderer's Electrical Supplies on the right. Courtesy City of Sunnyvale.

because she was a union organizer. The growers swayed public opinion in their favor by stressing the link between the union organizers and the Communist Party.[26] It was not until 1939 that cannery workers in Sunnyvale were successful in establishing a union under the AFL umbrella, while the dried fruit packers organized with the CIO.

By 1930, the city officials and town merchants recognized that total economic dependence on the fruit industry was subject to the weather, labor problems and precarious at best. Young George Wilhelmy, a school principal, became mayor in 1930 and he agreed with the general feeling that new industry, specifically the United States Navy with its new dirigible air fleet, would bring long-term stability to the local economy.

Chapter 4

MILITARY BUILDUP IN SUNNYVALE

Advances in aviation technology, an unexpected byproduct of the horrors of World War I, peaked American interest in Germany's aircraft-spotting Zeppelins, and two German airships were among war reparations from Germany. United States Navy Rear Admiral William A. Moffett aggressively lobbied the federal government to develop a fleet of state-of-the-art dirigible airships and contracts were awarded for the construction of two airships, the *Akron* to be stationed at Lakehurst, New Jersey, and the *Macon*, slated to be based somewhere on the West Coast.

The next order of business was to locate a site for a West Coast dirigible airbase. Newspapers chronicled the progress the Navy was making in its fleet development, and the articles caught the eye of Alameda County real estate agent Laura Thane Whipple. She had been trying to sell some grazing land belonging to Otto Hirsch in the Mountain View-Sunnyvale area which was a portion of the former *Rancho Yñigo*. Mrs. Whipple decided to have a first-hand look at the property and offered her elderly mother an afternoon drive to see the site. As she stood there on a sunny, clear November afternoon in 1928, looking out over the land, her increasingly impatient driving companion demanded to know what she saw. Quite simply Laura Whipple replied, "An airbase." She clambered onto the hood of her 1926 Dodge coupe, box camera in hand, and took a series of snapshots. Her excitement grew as she drove to Fremont where she took her idea to her client, Otto

Hirsch. They realized they would have to convince other property owners to sell portions of their land also in order to offer a large enough site to the Navy.

After a lengthy discussion, Whipple and Hirsch contacted Mountain View realtor William Wright and Sunnyvale's Rudolph Pederson. They were also intrigued by the idea and they recommended it to their respective chambers of commerce. Pederson and Wright knew the other property owners and were instrumental in aligning them to the cause. The largest portion of land was owned by Hirsch's Land Company. Merrill Lion owned another parcel which was leased to Fosgate-Lion Seed Company. Minnie and Antone Medeiros, also property owners, agreed to sell a portion of their land to offset financial obligations. The South Shore Port Company was willing to sell as was Henry Wong Him, a San Francisco businessman. The Holthouse family owned land directly adjacent to the proposed site, and they sold a piece to the project.

After mustering this local help, Whipple pasted her photos together in a panoramic view of the site and she sent them with her proposal to Washington, D. C. for consideration by the United States Navy.[1] Her plan was initially scoffed at by Navy officials, but undaunted, she enlisted the support of Congressman Arthur Free of Santa Clara County. Also at the urging of Laura Whipple, the San Francisco Junior Chamber of Commerce spearheaded the Northern California campaign to persuade the Navy to locate its new lighter-than-air base in Santa Clara County. Both Sunnyvale and county officials joined the regional effort along with chambers of commerce in San Francisco, Oakland, Mountain View and San José who also supported Whipple's endorsement of the site. The Bureau of Aeronautics, under Admiral Moffett, analyzed ninety-seven possible sites and the choice was narrowed down to two: Camp Kearney in San Diego and the thousand-acre site in Santa Clara County. The arduous process of choosing between San Diego and Santa Clara County would last almost three years.

Local promoters recognized that the only way to compete with the San Diego deal which offered the land free of charge to the Navy, was to do the same by raising funds to purchase the land outright from the landowners. The San Francisco Chamber pledged to raise a half-million dollars to purchase the property.[2] Fund-raising campaigns netted contributions from every town in the Bay Area including San José's pledge to raise $60,000 of the $100,000 quota for the county. Several county businessmen formed the Santa Clara Consolidated Air Base Committee to manage the fund drive, and local banker Charles Spalding represented Sunnyvale.[3]

Mrs. Whipple, along with realtors Wright and Pederson, convinced the various landowners to respond to an offer to purchase from the air base committee for approximately $450 per acre. After the selling price was negotiated, an escrow account was opened at San José Abstract and Title Company. Closing the sale of each parcel, except for those purchased outright by Otto Hirsch's Land Company, was contingent on the acceptance by the United States Navy of the land. The cash to pay the property owners came from the fund-raising campaigns around the bay and substantial donations by San Francisco businessmen.

A promotional film, featuring footage of Sunnyvale and the 1,000 acres as seen from the bay and the air, was made to convince Navy brass of the advantages of a Sunnyvale airbase. Promoters quickly realized it could be used to rally citizen support for the proposed base because it highlighted familiar surroundings while simultaneously raising needed cash. Residents flocked to theaters all over the Bay Area to see the film, and proceeds went to the fund-raising

effort. On May 23, 1930 the much ballyhooed film was shown at the Strand Theatre on Murphy Avenue in Sunnyvale, raising $70 to contribute to the effort.[4]

Laura Whipple worked diligently to convince local citizens and national politicians alike to choose the 1,000 acres in Sunnyvale as the site for the airbase. In a 1930 note to a personal friend Mrs. Whipple explained, "Since taking to the 'Air' I have not been fancy free . . . . The Air Work has simply made it impossible for me to concentrate on anything else."[5]

In the spring of 1930, representatives for the regional effort went to Washington, D.C. to urge Congress to approve the proposed base at Sunnyvale. Colonel Charles Lindbergh appeared at a secret session of the house committee and supported Sunnyvale as the location of a new airbase as well as an aeronautical research center.[6] The Sunnyvale site was chosen on December 12, 1930, generating such excitement that schools and businesses closed and impromptu parades formed. The placement of the base in the county would, people hoped, bring relief from financial hardships facing the valley.

With the land purchased, Representative Arthur Free introduced a bill in Congress to authorize government acceptance of the land and approval of an additional expenditure of $5 million for structures and development. The bill passed and was signed by President Hoover on February 20, 1931 and the land was transferred to the United States Navy at a cost of $1 on July 31, 1931.[7]

The location of the Naval Air Base in Sunnyvale met with very little opposition in Santa Clara County. The 1,000-acre site was actually located halfway between the towns of Sunnyvale and Mountain View. Early proponents suggested it be called Naval Air Station Mountain View-Sunnyvale, but Navy officials thought that the word "mountain" in the name would conjure images of mountainous peaks in the minds of congressmen back in Washington, D. C. In order to dispel any mental pictures of mountains or questions of flight safety, the Navy referred to the site as NAS Sunnyvale, a more pastoral-sounding name.[8]

Bay Area communities were proud of their combined effort and no small part of their enthusiasm was due to their victory over Southern California in the competition for the site. The regional organizing effort, a first for the Bay Area, was successful and Santa Clara Consolidated Air Base Committee chairman, Wendell Thomas, noted that

For the first time in the history of Northern California, we have learned the lesson of cooperation, and having learned this and profited by it greatly, it is certain we will act as a unit in the future on matters for the common good.[9]

Unfortunately, the regional cooperative effort was not often repeated in the decades ahead.

Laura Whipple took great pride in her involvement in the site selection of Moffett Field and her role was acknowledged by her contemporaries and the press. However, once the land was purchased and delivered to the Navy and construction began, Whipple's involvement diminished and her earlier efforts were largely forgotten. The Navy, how-

Mrs. Laura Thane Whipple (second from left) was honored by the Navy in 1962 for her part in the establishment of Moffett Field. Others pictured are (left to right) George Rolding, Jr., Mrs. Whipple, Mrs. Roland Bendel, and Mr. Newton Brury. Courtesy Gladys Williamson Collection, Alameda County Library, Fremont Main Library.

ever, did not forget the role that Mrs. Whipple played in the genesis of their base. In a special ceremony on September 28, 1962, Laura Whipple, then 87 years old, was presented with honorary United States Aviator Wings by base commander Captain George Clifford in recognition of her participation in the establishment of the base.[10]

The giant dirigible *Akron* visited the new air base on May 13, 1932, and it was greeted by tens of thousands of curious county residents. Close to 100,000 spectators jammed into Stanford Stadium in the predawn hours to get a glimpse of the mammoth airship.[11] Local authorities expected the spectacle to generate "the biggest traffic problem in state history" and went to great pains to publish maps in the press in an attempt to control crowds.[12]

In 1932 Arthur Free introduced another bill in Congress to appropriate $295,000 for an additional 700 acres adjacent to NAS Sunnyvale for an airplane landing field. The adjacent land involved another portion of the Holthouse ranch and Medeiros family property. Both families were offered $421 per acre, but they felt they should have been compensated the same as they had been for the earlier transaction: $450 per acre.

Ground-breaking had been in October 1931, and by the end of 1932, Hangar One was complete along with several other buildings. Hangar One, an elongated dome-like structure had "orange peel" doors mounted on rail tracks, stood eighteen stories high and covered eight acres. Total cost for construction was $2,250,000. The gigantic hangar, with its curved walls and ceilings, produced an eerie, disorienting optical illusion from inside. On the outside, it looked like a futuristic space station when the doors glided to open or close. Although the hangar is most conspicuous, the buildings surrounding Shenandoah Plaza near the main entrance to the base are also architecturally significant, partly because they are more reminiscent of mission-style than the structures at other military installations.

Naval Air Station Sunnyvale was commissioned by the Navy on April 12, 1933, but the festivities were overshad-

Airship Akron at Naval Air Station Sunnyvale, circa 1932. Courtesy Fred Marten to Sunnyvale Historical Society & Museum Association.

owed by disaster. Just a week earlier the *Akron* had crashed off the New Jersey coast killing 73 men, including Rear Admiral William Moffett. Not only was the "fleet" instantly cut in half by this accident, but the most experienced personnel were lost as well. It was a crushing blow to the fledgling dirigible program. The next month, on May 18, the landing field was designated Moffett Field in honor of Admiral Moffett. It was not until 1942 that the base was named NAS Moffett Field, one of only four Naval Air Stations to be named for a person rather than a geographical location.[13]

Later that year, on October 16, 1933, the *Macon* made its grand and long awaited appearance in the skies above the Santa Clara Valley. The *Macon* was a rigid airship, built with a vast aluminum framework, covered with a light-weight cotton fabric, then painted with six layers of airplane var-

nish. The massive dirigible measured 785 feet in length and 133 feet in diameter. The cavity held twelve separate helium gas cells with capacity of 6,500,000 cubic feet for helium to raise the ship. The nose sections held water ballasts which would be dumped to accelerate ascent.

Dirigibles acted as flying aircraft carriers and five Sparrowhawk fighter biplanes fit in the cavernous belly of the *Macon*. A giant hatch opened from the bottom and a crane-like "trapeze" lifted the planes in and out of the mother ship. The long-range scouts would return from a mission and hover below the hatch, like a hummingbird, until the "trapeze" lifted them inside. The next plane would follow the same procedure. The *Macon* could cover as many as 172,000 square miles in a day with the scouting planes in operation.

Aerial photo of Naval Air Station Sunnyvale with the USS Macon moored at the south circle, February 20, 1934. Official U. S. Navy Photograph, Courtesy Sunnyvale Historical Society & Museum Association.

Construction of Hangar One at Naval Air Station Sunnyvale, 1933. Courtesy San Jose Historical Museum.

The control car, about the size of a bus, hung from the belly side of the dirigible and contained navigation equipment, passenger seats and tables, bathrooms, and a kitchen. The crew and occasional passengers enjoyed incredible panoramic views from the windows completely surrounding the control car. The mighty structure, powered by eight 560-horsepower engines with attached propellers, housed as many as ninety crew members. Each engine was encased in a "gondola" large enough to accommodate the two required crew members to make any necessary in-flight repairs. Four giant fins, accessible from the inside of the dirigible, extended outside to provide steering. Electrically lighted internal walkways crisscrossed within the ship allowing accessibility to engine and airplane hatches, crew quarters and the control car.[14]

As the mighty airship silently floated toward its new home at Moffett Field that October day, farmers left their toil, children climbed on rooftops and people everywhere in the valley reverently watched the wondrous, colossal and magical beast make its way to the cavernous Hangar One. For the next eighteen months, the *Macon* became a more familiar sight in the skies over Santa Clara Valley as it went in and out for maneuvers, but the excitement and the wonder of it all never waned.

The *Macon* was initially commanded by Alger H. Dresel, and after fifteen months Lt. Commander Herbert V. Wiley took over. Since the crash of the *Akron*, Wiley and other dirigible proponents had been anxious to prove the capability of the huge airships. The ability to "search and locate" enemy ships far out at sea was their greatest asset. Wiley ordered the *Macon* out on an unauthorized search and locate mission in the Pacific. The target was the American cruiser *Houston*, whose passengers included none other than President Franklin Roosevelt on his way to Pearl Harbor. Implementing the sparrowhawk spotters, the *Macon* was able to locate the president 1,500 miles from land, and pilots of the little planes dropped mail and the latest newspapers to the amused president. The top Navy brass and crew of the *Houston* were not amused, however, and took a long while to recover from the shock of seeing airplanes, which looked to them like enemy bombers, approach their ship in the middle of the Pacific.[15]

Unfortunately, the following year, on February 12, 1935, while returning to Moffett Field after routine maneuvers and war games, the *Macon* encountered fierce winds off the Monterey coast. The upper tail fin was ripped from the airship, fatally puncturing three helium cells. Luckily, its descent to the sea was slow, enabling most of the crew to survive, and all but two of the eighty-one person crew were rescued. According to dirigible historian Basil Clarke, the *Macon* crash could have been avoided if the ship had been grounded earlier when a problem was first detected in the upper rudder fin. Clarke noted that proper repairs

would have meant grounding the ship for two months and this was considered to be unnecessary. Instead, the reinforced girders were put in piecemeal as and when opportunity offered, with the result that when Macon left the Naval Air Station at Sunnyvale, Calif., on 11th February 1935, to take part in a series of maneuvers over the Pacific both the elevator fins and the lower rudder fin had been strengthened but the upper rudder fin had not.[16]

The loss of the *Macon* in 1935 left America with one surviving dirigible, the German-made *Los Angeles*. When Germany's hydrogen-filled *Hindenberg* burned at Lakehurst, New Jersey in 1936, the lighter-than-air program completely collapsed.

The Navy traded Moffett Field to the Army in return for the Army's North Island base in San Diego on October 25, 1935, and the base was renamed "Moffett Field Army Air Corps Base." It was while Moffett Field was under jurisdiction of the Army that the National Advisory Committee for Aeronautics (NACA, later called the National Aeronautics

and Space Administration or NASA) opened its research facility, which was named Ames Aeronautical Laboratory in honor of Dr. Joseph Ames, past president of Johns Hopkins University and one time chairman of NACA.[17]

Construction projects at Moffett Field did provide many jobs for local workers in the early 1930s, but not enough to compensate for the steady stream of dust bowl migrants who flowed into California in search of work during this period. Their plight, brought into the national consciousness by John Steinbeck's The Grapes of Wrath, resulted from depressed crop prices and an extended drought in Oklahoma, Texas, Arkansas, and Louisiana. Two-and-a-half million people came to California during this period and Californians were not happy about this influx of impoverished migrants taking scarce Depression-era jobs. In 1934, however, Santa Clara County canners reported an all-time peak in their business.

Many Sunnyvale farmers hired migrant "Okies" to harvest their apricots, prunes and cherries to keep up with demand. Sunnyvale children looked forward to the arrival each harvest season of the "Okie" or Mexican migrant workers because they brought their children, new playmates for the season. Carole Pavlina's essay in Sunnyvale: City of Destiny explains, "The workers didn't always live in a tent or a cabin, but . . . they would build houses out of fruit trays which they could live in comfortably if it didn't rain."[18] Pavlina's description offers insight into the makeshift living arrangements of the transient Mexican and "Okie" orchard workers in Sunnyvale in the 1930s.

Hundreds of Italian-American families in the Sunnyvale area also struggled to survive the Depression. Some felt the government should offer more assistance to farmers as did the Italian government. The Sunnyvale Standard captured this sentiment when it ran a photo of the still popular Benito Mussolini riding a Caterpillar tractor claiming "Mussolini . . . is never too busy to attend any demonstration contributing to the benefit of the farmer . . . in Italy."[19] The newspaper praised the Italian government's support of farmers.

In an attempt to stay afloat in the turbulent economic tides of the 1930s, many local farmers sought work at the canneries and Hendy Iron Works in addition to maintaining their farms. Schuckl's Cannery founder Max Schuckl died in 1937, and employee Emil Rutz took over as president of the company. Rutz eventually served as president of California Processors and Growers, and after World War II, as president of the National Canners Association. Schuckl's Cannery operated on its thirty-one acres along the railroad in Sunnyvale, but its administration offices did not relocate from San Francisco until 1942. The new administration building was designed by architect William Wurster and was lauded as

> the most famous example of Wurster as an industrial architect . . . . Its redwood frame might be a sheet drawn taut, it is so slight, and the trellises over the horizontal window strips add accents so subtle that this is likely to be remembered as one of the incomparable business buildings of the twentieth century.[20]

Clearly the author of this accolade must have been mightily dismayed when the Fair Oaks overpass was built in the

William Wurster-designed Schuckl Cannery administration building, built in 1942 and razed in the 1980s. Courtesy California History Center, Stocklmeir Library/ Archives.

1960s, virtually eliminating visibility of the building, and ultimately when the building was torn down to build condominiums in the 1980s.

Joshua Hendy Iron Works had been purchased by a German-Jewish immigrant, Mr. Fredrick Bennerman some time after John Hendy's death, and Bennerman attempted to keep the factory open through the Depression even though contracts were few and far between. The plant produced giant gates and valves for both the Grand Coulee and Boulder (later renamed Hoover) dams. A former worker explained:

> Old timers recall how fortunate they were to be able to keep busy on their nearby farms and orchards while they waited to be summoned back to work [at the Iron Works]. When the whistle tooted vigorously during the day, they knew a new order had been received and they hurried back to the plant and their machines, ready to see what was to be done.[21]

Bennerman lost the Iron Works to the Bank of California in the late 1930s, but the bank kept the operation running until it was purchased in 1940.

Hendy Iron Works changed hands just before World War II and benefited tremendously by the war economy. Six construction companies which had participated in the construction of Boulder and Grand Coulee dams, among other projects, together formed a cartel. One member of the construction cartel, Charles Moore of Moore Machinery in San Francisco, became embroiled in litigation with Hendy in 1940. He went to Sunnyvale in an attempt to settle the issue and was surprised by the amount of equipment sitting idle. He called other cartel members, including W. A. "Dad" Bechtel, Felix Kahn, Henry Kaiser and John McCone, and suggested that the cartel purchase Hendy to sell the machinery for a fast profit. A timely tip from the Navy, however, encouraged Moore and Kahn to make a trip to Washington, D.C. to bid on government contracts on behalf of the cartel. Their military and political connections did indeed help to secure contracts and along with Henry Kaiser's help, won $10 million in Navy contracts with an additional $1.3 million for new facilities. The cartel bought Hendy Iron Works for $320,000 from the Bank of California.[22] What had begun as an idea to sell the plant for scrap metal turned into a multi-million dollar war production plant. The cartel ownership of Hendy Iron Works provided a huge influx of cash to up-grade the facility and hire new workers in time to meet wartime contract deadlines for Liberty Ship engines.

The bombing of Pearl Harbor changed the course of history in California and radically altered the lives of many who lived in Santa Clara County and Sunnyvale. A month after Pearl Harbor was attacked, Japanese-Americans and "enemy aliens" in Sunnyvale were directed to surrender personal property that was considered war-related. The items included:

> *firearms, weapons or implements of war or component parts thereof, ammunition, bombs, explosives or material used in the manufacture of explosives, shortwave radio receiving sets, transmitting sets, signal devices, codes or ciphers and cameras.*[23]

Former Fremont High School student and football player Ben Aihara enlisted in the Army a few days after the bombing of Pearl Harbor. Aihara, the American-born son of Japanese immigrants, reported for training at Jefferson Barracks, Missouri. Racist sentiment toward local Japanese residents pervaded Sunnyvale even though Japanese-American men joined the United States armed forces. The town passed a formal resolution proclaiming its distrust of the Japanese and its "ban of Japs permanently from our City and State."[24] This resolution remained on the books in Sunnyvale until 1989, when local Japanese-Americans brought it to the attention of the city council who unanimously voted to remove it from city regulations.

Many residents of Sunnyvale felt that their town would be a particular target for Japanese attack because of nearby Moffett Field, the armament production at Hendy

Iron Works, and makeshift Army recruit training grounds at Washington Park and Fremont High School. Fear of attack perpetuated anti-Japanese feeling that gripped the entire West Coast and early in 1942 curfew rules were enforced in Sunnyvale. "All Japanese, Germans, Italians and persons of Japanese ancestry residing in Sunnyvale must be within their place of residence between the hours of 8 p.m. and 6 a.m. daily."[25] It is unclear whether these restrictions were ever enforced for any of the "enemy aliens" other than the Japanese. The justification for separation of Japanese-Americans from their possessions, property, and the community was the supposed likelihood of a Japanese attack on the West Coast and fear of spying, sabotage, and other acts of disloyalty.

On February 19, 1942, Executive Order 9066 authorized internment camps and directed all residents on the West Coast of Japanese ancestry incarcerated for the duration of the war. Ben Aihara's parents were interned while their son served in the United States Army. Some of Sunnyvale's growers urged that the sanctions against the Japanese be delayed until spring, not in defense of their neighbors, but so farm work would be complete in preparation for that year's crop. Likewise in 1945, at the end of the war, the returning Japanese were quickly hired to harvest that season.

The outbreak of war initiated coastal patrols by the Navy to search for enemy submarines and mines. Non-rigid airships, or blimps, were the best means of patrolling, and Moffett Field's huge hangar, which was under-utilized by the Army, could easily house them. On April 15, 1942 the base was returned to the Navy and recommissioned NAS Sunnyvale and four days later renamed NAS Moffett Field. The management change generated numerous contracts for military buildup.

In 1942 Hendy Iron Works bought out Sunnyvale's Hydro-Carbon Company, a turn-of-the-century business started with investments from local farmers. The take-over was authorized by an Office of Production Management directive that Hydro-Carbon's production of varnish,

LEFT: *Front cover of* Iron Men, *a publication for the employees of Hendy Iron Works during World War II, 1943. Courtesy Sunnyvale Historical Society & Museum Association.*

BELOW: *Woman worker at Hendy Iron Works during World War II. Courtesy Sunnyvale Historical Society & Museum Association.*

Nat King Cole performs at noontime rally for employees at Hendy Iron Works during World War II. Courtesy Sunnyvale Historical Society & Museum Association.

lacquer and waxes was "non-essential" to the war effort. Sunnyvale, however, was declared a "Critical Defense Area" because of Hendy and Moffett Field, so it was the only town on the San Francisco peninsula allowed to build houses. Samuel Hyman, a construction contractor in San Francisco, was allowed to begin construction on 250 houses on thirty eight acres of pear and apricot orchards at Fair Oaks and California avenues, adjacent to the Iron Works. Only 55 two and three-bedroom homes were actually built, but the

neighborhood came to be known as "Victory Village" where Hendy workers bought houses for about $6,000.

Under the direct management of cartel member Charles Moore, business at the Iron Works began to boom. The plant was in production twenty-four hours a day and their slogan "What America needs, Hendy can build" served to inspire all the workers. It became like a little city, producing Iron Men magazine and developing its own police and fire departments. Even a full-time barber was hired. The workers identified themselves as the "Iron Men of Hendy" even though women worked in the plant as well. The war effort had the unusual effect of bringing together the most unlikely of coworkers: housewives, businessmen, farmers, music teachers, and bakers. Joseph McKiernan's "Song of the Iron Men," reprinted in the Iron Men magazine, expressed the attitude that was sweeping the nation:

We're the Iron men of Hendy
and sons of liberty
And every ship that rides the sea
has a part of you and me.
We're the Iron men of Hendy
all pledged to loyalty
We'll never let a day go by
that won't sock the axis in the eye.[26]

During World War II, one-and-a-half million military personnel passed through the Port of San Francisco on their way to or from the war in the Pacific. Men from all areas of the United States saw California for the first time, and many eventually came back after the war to live. Besides servicemen, thousands of defense industry workers came to the Bay Area, and specifically to Sunnyvale where they worked at Joshua Hendy Iron Works or Moffett Field.

Harry Gunetti, hired as Hendy plant manager, initiated a renewed effort to perfect the mass production of the gigantic marine steam engines, each weighing 140 tons and standing close to 25 feet tall. In three-and-a-half years, beginning in 1942, Hendy Iron Works turned out a record

754 Liberty Ship engines. During 1944, Hendy workers produced 252 "Tiny Tim" rocket launchers in a single week. Secret engineering research and development went on throughout the war on the Hendy property in conjunction with Stanford University and local engineering consulting firms. One secret project team developed the Sky Sweeper, a three-inch diameter, 70 caliber, double-barreled deck-mounted machine gun intended to shoot down kamikazi dive bombers before they were able to damage American ships. It was designed by two Stanford professors, a conveyor expert from Libby canneries, two engineers from Schlage Lock Company and some men from Hendy Iron Works. Unknown even to the engineers on the project, Hendy produced parts for the first twenty-five Sky Sweepers, although by the time of production the war was over.[27]

The work force at Hendy swelled from 60 employees in 1940 to 7,500 by the end of the war. The insatiable hunger of the military and defense industries created serious labor shortages for California agriculture, including Sunnyvale's fruit orchards. For the first time, Mexicans were hired at canneries, an unprecedented opportunity to get out of the fields. One Mexican woman, Elena Robles, recalled the war era when Mexicans could get work in Sunnyvale that was not restricted to the orchards: "Up to this time [the War], the canneries, . . . had never hired Mexicans full time. They hired Italians and other ethnic groups, but rarely hired Mexicans or Blacks. Now they needed manpower."[28]

Local farmers recognized the needs of the nation's war machine, but they also hoped to be able to survive themselves. Their desperate demands for workers encouraged the United States government, in cooperation with the Mexican government, to negotiate wages and conditions to import Mexican contract farm workers to keep California's agriculture business afloat for the duration of the war. The Bracero Program, (literally "arms," referring to manual labor) intended to be in effect only for the duration of the war, was ultimately extended until 1964. The Secretary of Labor had the authority to import and export Mexican workers as needed and the availability of workers provided by the Bracero Program gave growers the leverage to continue high production while keeping wages low.[29]

Negotiation of wages was carried out at first by the Farm Security Administration, and later by the War Food Administration. Efforts were made to mollify California's labor unions that opposed importation of Mexican laborers, but in reality, the federal government actively controlled wage levels and labor under the guise of preserving California's agricultural economy. Impoverished conditions in Mexico and the availability of jobs for untrained workers in California also encouraged the immigration of Mexican workers who hoped to escape lifelong poverty in Mexico.

Playwright Luis Valdez was the son of Mexican farmworkers who wanted California to be their land of opportunity. They labored in Sunnyvale fields during World War II and one day, while picking tomatoes with his parents, six-year-old Luis Valdez spied a blimp silently floating toward Moffett Field:

> At that instant, something caught my eye, and I looked up at the sky. My cry came out as I spotted this huge blimp heading for one of those giant hangars at Moffett Field . . . it was a magical place, with airships floating through the sky and landing. Even as a farmworker, as a child, I felt privileged to be in this magic land.[30]

The child eyes overlooked the demanding life of the migratory farm worker life.

By 1943, war-related industry was the dominant economic factor in Sunnyvale, usurping the pre-eminence of the fruit industry. The expectation of a national recession at the end of the war caused local officials to voice concern about the postwar economy in Sunnyvale. The common assumption, however, was that the economy would once again become fruit-centered. Women would return to seasonal cannery work and their homes, while men would grow and harvest fruit. The braceros were to return to Mexico, never to be needed again. The Japanese could come back as long as they would contribute to the farming venture.

These assumptions had proven erroneous by 1946. Some women workers who had obtained war jobs outside of the home and canneries had no intention of returning to housework. Many farmers' sons found they could make a better living in industry. Returning GIs faced job scarcity by filling Bay Area college campuses for an education that would previously have been unavailable to them. Mexican farmworkers had become dependent on the work and needed to return every season to support their families in Mexico, and for some, California was appealing as a permanent residence. A few Japanese in Santa Clara County were able to reclaim their property in 1945; most had to rebuild new lives from scratch.

Before the war, the economy of California and the entire West was colonial in nature, dependent on the East for goods and services. From 1941 to 1945, however, the federal government pumped $35 billion dollars into California industry to fuel the war machine. Historian Gerald Nash points out that "as no other single event in the history of the West, the war stimulated economic growth. The erstwhile colony emerged from the war as an economic pace-setter for the nation."[31] Although the federal government was not the only impetus for economic change in the West, it was the most significant factor.

The underdeveloped economy of pre-war California turned out to be a fertile environment for new and innovative businesses, particularly aerospace and electronics. There was no formal infrastructure of corporate bureaucracy as in the East to impede the growth of new technologies. The federal dollars allowed new research in nuclear energy, aviation, and shipbuilding.[32]

After the war, disputes arose among cartel Hendy owners resulting in a buy-out of Charles Moore's interest in Hendy Iron Works. He was replaced by John McCone, president of California Shipbuilding Corporation. Westinghouse Corporation, which had contracted with Hendy on many projects throughout the war, began exhibiting interest in the management of the plant. It put together a bid to buy the company.

Flight research continued at NACA despite a personnel shortage during the war, and they built wind tunnels to test airplane drag, anti-turbulence devices, dive controls, and developed de-icing techniques. The fighting airplanes that helped win the war were maintained and improved with the help of Ames Laboratory. Their new designs came out toward the end of the war, and set America on the path toward the supersonic age.

The foundation had been laid for further industrial and technological growth in the San Francisco Bay Area and Sunnyvale. The effort to produce more efficient war machines was translated into the private sector by Stanford-educated engineers who had worked on defense products and now began to search for ways to make a living with their research experience in private industry. The permanent presence of the military at Moffett Field also ensured future defense department contracts.

The economic and social disruption of the Depression, with the upheaval of World War II following closely on its heels, had lasting consequences for California, the San Francisco Bay Area, and thus for Sunnyvale. The Depression and war eras mark the beginning of active solicitation of and economic dependence on military contracts and the business of war. They also mark the beginning of the end of family-run commercial orchards in Santa Clara County.

Chapter 5

FAREWELL TO FARMS

The Japanese surrender in August of 1945 halted war production throughout the nation. At Sunnyvale's Hendy Iron Works almost eight thousand workers were let go. A sense of foreboding about the economy both nationally and locally overshadowed euphoria at the war's end. Hendy's cutbacks sparked fears and residents and business people gathered in December 1945 to organize a more active chamber of commerce and form a search committee to recruit applicants for a manager of the reorganized chamber. The Iron Works was up for sale and the owners had solicited bids from potential buyers, among them Westinghouse Corporation, a major supplier to the defense department. The chamber, overrun with questions about the Hendy facility and the town, hoped that its reorganization would present solutions and draw new business to town.

The following summer Sunnyvale's Chamber of Commerce hired Navy veteran Al Spiers, recently a chamber manager in a southern California town. Sunnyvale city fathers, with the help of Spiers, conceived and executed an active and organized strategy to recruit industry in hopes of averting economic decline. When Spiers arrived he realized many townspeople did not share his vision for a booming Sunnyvale. His most formidable opponents were antigrowth orchardists whose interest was not so much to keep people out as to keep the city from exercising power over their land and lives. Spiers tried to be diplomatic with the farming community by using terms like "economic development" and "industrial parks." Farmers saw impending doom for themselves despite Spiers' attempts to enlist their support.[1]

Westinghouse Corporation took over the operation of Hendy's in the spring of 1947 with a ten-year lease and option to purchase. At the end of 1948 the company exercised the option, buying "the largest electrical manufacturing plant in the entire West" for almost $4,000,000. The cartel's 1940 investment of $320,000 paid off handsomely.

The facility was upgraded with an electrical power

Rally in yard of Hendy Iron Works on VJ Day in 1945. Courtesy Joseph Donovan to Sunnyvale Historical Society & Museum Association.

sub-station equal to that supplying the entire town of Sunnyvale. Some areas of the forty-year old plant, however, still had dirt or wood floors and major renovations were necessary. Postwar products at the former Hendy Iron Works included high-speed color printing presses for Life and Time magazines, hydraulic gates and valves, the Richmond-Chase Prune Packaging Machine, and various weapons systems like the Sky Sweeper and the Air Force Tullahoma Axial Flow Compressors. Westinghouse positioned itself in Sunnyvale to be ready and available for production in the aftermath of the war.

When Westinghouse bought the Hendy plant, the general manager explained in a letter to Al Spiers that the company had decided to settle in Sunnyvale only in part because of the existing Hendy facility. Other important factors were:

> *interest of the community in bringing large industry*
> *into this area, the fine reception given them by Mayor*
> *Raines, the offer of cooperation by Banker Les*
> *Harriman, and the contributions made by your*
> *Chamber of Commerce . . . .*[2]

Spiers' crusade to transform Sunnyvale from a farm town to an industrial city coalesced with the decision by Westinghouse to locate in Sunnyvale. From his first office, a converted girls' restroom in McKinley School, he preached long and loud to convert non-believers to his faith of industrial growth.

Dramatic changes occurred simultaneously throughout California in the postwar period. The West no longer identified itself as a sleepy frontier but as a hotbed of economic activity critical to the whole nation. Cities and towns in this era launched extensive city planning projects in accordance with the emerging idea that the West was on the verge of a new age. Historian Gerald Nash noted that "hundreds of these western towns and cities thus created postwar development commissions whose task it was to transform western dreams into realities on the local level."[3]

In Sunnyvale, one of the first orders of business was to restructure the local government in order to facilitate prompt decision and action. Early in 1949, the board of freeholders drew up a city charter which delineated a new chain of command in local government. The most fundamental change called for in the proposed charter was the creation of a city executive or city manager. The city council would act as a policy-making board of directors and appoint the city manager. The executive would actually manage the city and appoint subordinate department heads. The council would maintain jurisdiction over the manager, but not over the appointed department heads. In addition, the charter called for a system of initiative, referendum and recall, which mirrored the procedures in the Elections Code of California.

The few vocal opponents objected more to specific clauses, such as authorization of revenue bonds, than to the charter itself. Mayor Webber urged citizens to attend the public meetings to discuss the charter. "It is your duty as a citizen of Sunnyvale to give the Freeholders the benefit of your opinion at this series of meetings."[4] The first town meeting drew only seventy-five citizens whose primary complaint was that there were not enough copies of the charter available at public places for people to read. The full text of the charter was published in the next issue of the Sunnyvale Standard, and the following meeting drew only forty residents. The Standard clearly favored charter city status:

> *Of course, it [the charter] could be voted down, which*
> *would negate the months of work of the Freeholders,*
> *and keep our city operating under the present*
> *restrictive, 'small town' laws that most Sunnyvalans*
> *[sic], we feel sure, are trying to escape.*[5]

An election was held on May 10, 1949, and the charter was approved 398 to 276. Only 21% of the 3,209 eligible voters cast a ballot. A mere 122 votes set the course for Sunnyvale's future development. A municipal election was held on August 16, 1949, and the top five vote-getters became the first city council under the new charter. Both the May and August elections indicate Sunnyvale's choice to grow beyond a small town. If opponents had mobilized an opposition effort, they could have easily defeated the charter with greater voter turnout.

Acceptance of the charter signaled a transition from the old, comfortable, slightly tattered Sunnyvale to a shiny, new and modern city. This pivotal point in Sunnyvale's history marks a redistribution of power which disfranchised the former town fathers and the farming community. While the disappearance of family farms was bemoaned in the late 1960s and early 1970s as if it were a new phenomenon, this 1949 election set the town on a decidedly pro-growth path with virtually no room for agricultural endeavor.

The first city manager hired by the city council was University of California graduate H. K. (Ken) Hunter. He, in turn, hired Caroline Ryan as his secretary and she remained on the city staff until the 1980s. Hunter was filled with the latest ideas on municipal government. He wrote and published articles in professional journals detailing his thoughts on local government, bringing attention to Sunnyvale's emerging system of government and to Hunter himself. His work on public safety issues was particularly well-received.[6]

Ken Hunter was an outspoken advocate for combining Sunnyvale's police and fire-fighting resources into a single Department of Public Safety. Mayor Walt Jones also favored the consolidation, but feared negative political fallout from such a decision. The strongest and most vocal opposition to the new concept came from the Sunnyvale volunteer fire fighters, and they rallied public support for their position. Nevertheless, on July 1, 1950, Sunnyvale's City Council approved the integration of police and fire fighters into one department, becoming the first city in the nation to do so and prompting the mass resignation of the entire squad of volunteers. The forward-thinking plan ultimately saved the residents money in fire insurance premiums and saved the city money in operating two

separate departments. The new department had three divisions: police patrol, fire division and staff serving both. All public safety officers were called for emergencies but a minimal number were on active duty at any particular time.

Twenty-six candidates applied and were tested for the new position of director of public safety, only five passing the exam. Jacob Jessup of Washington state was hired and remained in the position for twenty years. Both Jessup and Hunter felt that their biggest obstacle to implementation of the new department was "tradition" in Sunnyvale. There were hard feelings when the volunteers disbanded and emotionally charged criticism continued for many years to come.

Subtler changes also resulted from the adoption of the city charter and the new-fangled ideas of town management coming in from the outside. City Manager Hunter's perception of the town, "an industrial city,"[7] was clearly different from that of many longtime townspeople. A heretofore well-defined community identity, grounded in agriculture, began to be dismantled as traditional methods of civic participation were radically altered. Elimination of the volunteer fire department was one clear example. True, population growth demanded an economical yet effective system of protective services. What went unacknowledged,

Sunnyvale volunteer fire fighters, circa 1920s. Courtesy California History Center, Stocklmeir Library/Archives.

however, was the community service and spirit generated over decades that the volunteers, now relegated to the back shelf, had offered the town. Since its inception, the volunteer fire corps had over 130 members, many of whom were fathers and sons, brothers and cousins who met formally and informally to discuss town issues. Not only had they fought fires, but they sponsored parades and Christmas parties for children, built an outdoor volleyball court and started a softball team. Unfortunately, their service and contributions to the community were not incorporated into the future-oriented policies of the city. Longtime volunteer fire fighter and Murphy Avenue barber Billy Wetterstrom admitted that he sometimes "left a customer in the chair" if the fire alarm sounded. The volunteers continued to meet for a long time after they were disbanded as Wetterstrom recalled, "All the men opposed the new paid force. . . . The closeness among the volunteers remained after they were replaced. They would meet regularly and talk about the 'good times.'" Another lifelong volunteer and former Mayor Emile Corboline explained that if a fire occurred, a siren would sound to call the volunteers to the firehouse. The men kept their own fire fighting jumpsuit and equipment at home. Corboline claimed "Everyone wanted to help out. It was a real honor."[8]

The former mayors and town trustees also found themselves on the outside looking in. Of the city council members elected in August of 1949, only William Theller had served previously. Incumbent Sam Wright was voted out as he received five hundred fewer votes than the lowest vote-getter of the new council, Ernest M. Stout. Evidence of a changing of the guard became very clear when commissions were appointed in September. The seven-member planning commission had two holdovers from the previous term. The five-member Department of Parks and Recreation had none of the former parks commissioners. The five-member building code board of appeals maintained only one member of the earlier board. Walter Jones served as mayor until 1953 and Hunter held the city manager position until 1958. Bill Gilmore, former Schuckl's cannery worker and founder

of Sunnyvale Lumber was elected to city council in this transition period and he served a term as mayor in the mid-1950s.

The reorganized chamber and the new city council specifically stated that they did not want Sunnyvale to become a bedroom community for San Francisco or San José. Many residents, however, were happy to live in a quiet, agricultural town. Hunter and Spiers created a structure to encourage industrial growth alongside residential development. There was no plan, however, to account for or include agriculture which heretofore had been the economic and social backbone of the town. Sunnyvale and other Santa Clara County towns attempted to reach beyond agriculture to embrace a more diversified economy.

Mother Nature, as though aware of the winds of change sweeping Sunnyvale, kicked up her own storm on a January morning in 1951 when residents were caught off guard as 100 mile winds whipped through town and a tornado touched down, damaging numerous buildings and homes in the northwest section of town. No one was killed that Thursday morning, but nerves were rattled by the gale-force winds that ripped porches and roofs off of several homes with damage to the town estimated at $1 million. Westinghouse suffered the loss of portions of two buildings on their grounds and estimated the damage to be in the neighborhood of $250,000 and Sunnyvale's Southern Pacific Depot was completely destroyed. The next day, in a Sunnyvale Standard person on-the-street interview, citizens were asked if efforts should be made to salvage the depot building. To a one, all agreed it had been an eyesore before the tornado, and the damage gave a good excuse to replace it.[9]

The mid-1950s offered a unique opportunity to local and county governments in the Santa Clara Valley to allow controlled growth and maintain a balanced economy promoting industry while preserving the agricultural base. Each municipality, however, implemented their own separate development and zoning codes, thereby missing an opportunity to coordinate regional planning strategies. While regional cooperation had been the hallmark of the

Tornado damage in Sunnyvale, January 1951. Courtesy Sunnyvale Historical Society & Museum Association.

1930s in the establishment of Moffett Field, brutal competition between towns prevailed during the 1950s. Local governments engaged in greedy land-grabbing and did not perceive the need to protect agricultural land. Pandemonium broke out in municipal annexation battles causing hundreds of farmers to choose between selling to reap the

financial benefits, or attempting to farm in an increasingly suburban area.

San José, the largest city in Santa Clara County, began to stretch out its boundaries in an attempt to become the "Los Angeles of the north" and to create a larger tax base. After World War II, Anthony "Dutch" Hamann was hired as San José's city manager. He and his aides became known as Dutch Hamann's "panzer division" because of the way they plowed through farms attempting to convince landowners of the benefits and inevitability of annexation. The official attitude was unreservedly pro-growth as described in Philip Trounstine and Terry Christensen's 1982 analysis of political power in communities:

> *The city government wanted to give developers and landowners what they needed, but they also wanted to make strategic annexations that would maintain San José's dominance of the valley, "bottling up" other cities rather than being trapped by them. The city manager's "Panzer Division" was vigorously engaged in urban imperialism, at war with neighboring communities.*[10]

Hamann justified his policies with the idea that expansionism was a civic "survival of the fittest" and was "meant to be." One researcher called it "municipal manifest destiny" at work, whereby aggressive action was justified for the supposed greater good.[11]

Sunnyvale, like San José, was particularly aggressive in its quest for broader city limits. Up to 1950, only sixty-seven acres had been added to the town and the population had gradually increased to just under 10,000. When Sunnyvale had incorporated in 1912, the town measured almost six square miles and founder Walter Crossman had specifically included within the town boundaries a narrow strip of land leading to the bay in hopes of establishing Port Sunnyvale. According to 1950s county regulations, property directly contiguous to existing town boundaries was the only land that could be annexed. Crossman's narrow strip of land enabled thousands of acres to be quickly and legally annexed to Sunnyvale. Chamber Manager Al Spiers credited Crossman's foresight for the industrial development of the 1950s and 1960s. It is highly unlikely, however, that Crossman, ever in his wildest dreams, envisioned the present-day 25-square-mile Sunnyvale.

Litigation resulted from annexation proceedings initiated by several Santa Clara County towns, including Sunnyvale. Cupertino filed a petition for incorporation in 1954 to protect itself from being swallowed up by Sunnyvale and San José. That same year Santa Clara filed suit against Sunnyvale claiming that annexed property along Lawrence Station Road "illegally spilled into Santa Clara territory."[12] Eighteen separate annexation proceedings were filed by Sunnyvale in 1956. The two largest parcels represented land earmarked for Lockheed (Guadalupe tract, no. 2 at 265 acres) and General Motors (Manzanita tract, no. 1, at 238 acres).[13] Valuable tax revenues to be generated by these corporations motivated the city to initiate proceedings before neighboring towns could do so. Mountain View filed suit against Sunnyvale for its annexation of the Lockheed land, but Judge Edwin Owens ruled in favor of Sunnyvale. His opinion stated that Sunnyvale had followed correct procedure for annexation, even though the land in question had previously been served by the Mountain View School District.[14]

The whirlwind of annexations by the City of Sunnyvale during the 1950s was perceived as heroic by the chamber of commerce, unfair by other municipalities, and downright criminal by many farmers. By 1957, Sunnyvale encompassed thirteen-and-a-half square miles. Table 1 indicates the number of acres annexed to Sunnyvale from 1950 to 1956.

In an effort to preserve their farms, orchardists convinced the county government to amend the zoning ordinance to include "exclusive agriculture." But municipal governments feared that farmers had them in a stranglehold that would not allow them to expand so they began to annex land to get around the county ordinance.[15] In 1955, the California State Legislature passed the "Agricultural Exclu-

sion Act" which stipulated that land zoned by a county for exclusive agriculture could not be annexed by a city without the consent of the owner. City governments raced to annex thousands of acres of property in the ninety days before the law took effect. Ultimately, the suburban and industrial growth that Al Spiers had predicted as inevitable became a

Table 1

NUMBER OF ACRES ANNEXED BY SUNNYVALE 1950-1956

1950	65
1951	269
1952	989
1953	1,003
1954	505
1955	1,251
1956	1,093

Source: Sunnyvale Standard, January 9, 1957, p. 1

reality. The farmers sold, speculators built, and the cities had difficulty in paying for the amenities that they had promised to all. Farmers put up considerable resistance, but they were unsuccessful in their bid to keep themselves outside the city limits and curtail rampant annexation.

By the summer of 1954, twenty-nine residential housing developments with four thousand houses valued at $18 million were under construction in Sunnyvale. Table 2 indicates residential developments as of August, 1954.

Some Sunnyvale residents developed their own

Table 2

HOUSING DEVELOPMENTS IN SUNNYVALE, 1954

Arbor Court	Greenvale Manor	Oak Manor
Arleen Manor	Holiday Manor	Orchard Gardens
Bayview Haven	Karville Manor	Parkside Manor
Carroll Gardens	La Linda Dell	Sunnyside Manor
Cherry Chase	La Linda Park	Sunnyvale Acres
Cherry Estates	La Linda Terrace	Sunnyvale Terrace
Fair Oaks Park	Lawrence Manor	Walnut Park
Gavello Glen	Madrone Manor	Western Estates
Greenwood Manor	Manzanita Park	Westmoor Village

Source: San Francisco Chronicle, August 15, 1954, p. 2(L).

land. Matt and Mary Miholovich, for example, bought five acres and built a house for themselves while developing the remaining lots. Later they bought an additional five acres in partnership with another local resident, Oscar Liebert. They developed Bay View Haven "way out in the boondocks," near Old San Francisco Road and Fair Oaks, into twenty-nine lots measuring from 8,800 square feet to 19,000 square feet. The lots, advertised in the San Francisco Chronicle, were priced from $4,400 to $5,000 and four lots sold even before the street paving began.[16] Miholovich was a local cement contractor who left his stamp on hundreds of Sunnyvale public works projects and the foundations of schools and industrial buildings.

Eichler homes were built in Sunnyvale from the end of World War II up to the early 1960s. Builder Joseph Eichler sought to build affordable tract houses using modern, architecturally designed plans. The houses featured exposed wood construction and a glassed-in garden terrace in the center of the house. The flat-topped homes give the impression of being larger than they are because of the extensive use of glass. Eichler homeowner Ann Hines noted, "Eichler liked to claim he was one of the first to add the 'family room,' a standard feature in homes today. His adoption of the family room living space, together with his merging of indoor/outdoor environments through use of the central atrium court plan . . . " emphasized his concern for quality of life within the home.[17] Other trademarks of Eichler homes were the use of radiant heat where warmth emanates evenly from floor to ceiling, and the concrete slab floor which eliminated the need for a traditional foundation and basement.

Gavello Glen homes near El Camino Real and Wolfe Road, bear some similarities to Eichlers. They sit on quarter-acre lots, emphasizing privacy, and feature extensive use of redwood on the interior. These houses won the Merit Award from the American Institute of Architects' "Homes For Better Living" contest in 1956. After four Gavello Glen houses sold to a developer who intended to build seven homes in their place in the late 1980s, neighborhood homeowners formed an association to try to save the neighborhood's houses. The group succeeded in galvanizing neighbors to raise the consciousness of city officials about saving older neighborhoods.

Three-bedroom tract houses built in Westmoor Village by corporate developer Holiday Homes replaced the eighty-acre D'Arrigo orchard. Every lot had mature fruit trees; the subdivision ads proclaimed "country living" because of the "built-in orchard." Mary Avenue bisected the property and the Mary-El Shopping Center was built at the edge of the tract on El Camino Real. Cherry Chase was developed by the joint efforts of several builders, including W. C. Garcia, Sunset Homes, McKenzie & Crawford, Arnesen Construction and Mann Construction. Cherry Chase homes were "tailored to the tastes of junior executives." The average lot size was 6,000 square feet with prices ranging from $11,950 to $13,950. McKenzie & Crawford, the biggest contractor in Cherry Chase, constructed 223 homes in three-and-a-half months and most were sold before completion. Cherry Chase Shopping Center on El Camino Real was developed by San Francisco builder James Arnott, in conjunction with Rogers Development Corporation, adjacent to the 1,400 Cherry Chase homes.

Many of today's Santa Clara County residents, and particularly those in Sunnyvale's Lakewood neighborhood, would be surprised to learn that there was an airport on 250 acres at Lawrence Expressway, just north of the Bayshore Freeway. The Santa Clara Valley Airport was established shortly after World War II by about ten investors who pooled cash to buy the land and have it graded for a runway. They built a mechanics' shop near the taxi strip, and a small office building where, over coffee after their flights, the pilots and passengers would engage in "hangar flying," rehashing the great moments of their adventures in the air. Harriet and Harold Willson, son and daughter-in-law of the famed walnut farmer Frank Chapman Willson, along with Dr. Diesner and several others, were among a number of amateur pilots who formerly had to drive to Palo Alto Airport to fly. The runway so close to home was a great coup for the

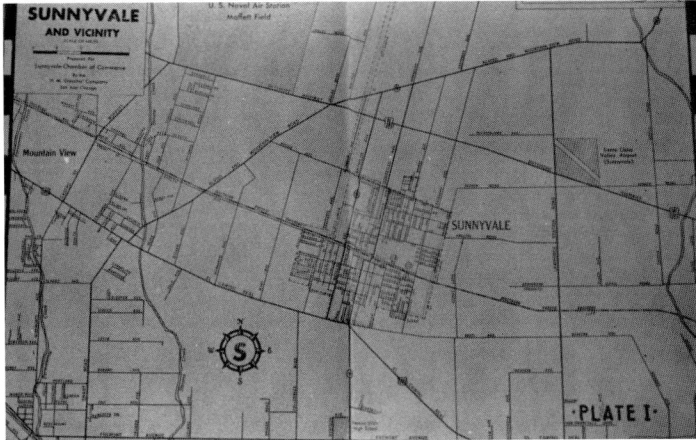

Map of Sunnyvale, circa 1950. Note the Santa Clara Valley Airport top right. Courtesy Sunnyvale Chamber of Commerce to Sunnyvale Historical Society & Museum Association.

Harold Willson leans on his plane at Santa Clara Valley Airport near today's Lawrence Expressway and Highway 101, circa 1950. Courtesy Harriet Willson to Sunnyvale Historical Society & Museum Association.

aviation buffs. The enterprise was fairly shortlived, however, and the property was sold and developed by 1955.[18]

Greenvale Manor, the largest subdivision in Sunnyvale on a 130-acre tract, was also the farthest from the town center, with its location bounded by Reed Lane and Bowers Avenue. The 726 two and three-bedroom homes were priced from $8,300 to $9,000. Multiple family housing was also constructed in this period, and by 1957 thirteen acres of the Azevedo property north of Duane Avenue was the largest multi-family development in Sunnyvale with clusters of duplex, triplex and apartment buildings.

Federally insured mortgage programs, initiated to help new home buyers, worked also to market large-scale residential developments. The newspaper ads for Sunnyvale's growing residential tracts noted the availability of FHA and VA insured mortgages. Buyers sometimes benefited from the mortgage system, but developers successfully used the programs as marketing tools to promote their own product. The federal government therefore, was also an active participant in the unchecked growth in Sunnyvale and throughout California.[19]

The city council claimed that Sunnyvale was the first city in California to develop a "Controlled Industrial Area" which pre-zoned industrial land to the exclusion of residential development.[20] They put in streets and sewers using pay-as-you-go bonds. The council wanted incoming industries to be "clean" and enforced stipulations against smokestacks. Some companies seeking to locate in Sunnyvale's industrial area were turned away. Al Spiers imagined "industrial parks with a country club atmosphere, where employees can be happy without the bother of smoke and parking problems."[21]

The chamber of commerce actively recruited industry after World War II by advertising the town in national newspapers, including the Wall Street Journal.[22] Many large Eastern companies were already in the process of relocating to the West Coast because of population growth in California. Personal Products Corporation, a subsidiary of Johnson & Johnson, built a new facility in Sunnyvale in 1953. George Murphy, company president, said the move was "pure and simple economics." It was more cost effective to build a facility in California than to incur the cost of shipping products to growing populations.[23] Sunnyvale's business community put itself in a position to welcome new companies to the town. By 1952, ten new companies had joined the four that had survived the end of World War II. The city boasted an industrial payroll of $32,000,000. The companies new to Sunnyvale included Bowser Inc., R. H. Hamilton Co., Duncan Smith Co., Thorton Mills Co., Illuminitronic Engineering Co., Kaiser Aluminum and Chemical Corp., and Sylvania Electric Company.

The most important model for Sunnyvale's approach to industrial development was Stanford Industrial Park, the brain-child of Stanford University Engineering Professor Fred Terman. He envisioned

> *a community of technical scholars . . . . Such a community is composed of industries using highly sophisticated technologies, together with a strong university that is sensitive to the creative activities of the surrounding industry. This pattern appears to be the wave of the future.*[24]

Terman particularly advocated an environment for successful research and development of electronic products in the West to encourage his most gifted students to remain active at Stanford and keep graduates from going to Boston and MIT. However, stipulations made by Leland Stanford about "the Farm" prohibited the sale of land for any reason, including industrial development. Stanford Industrial Park, the first of its kind, was created in the 1950s by long-term land leases to high-technology companies thereby realizing Terman's dream while at the same time allowing "the Farm" to remain intact. Buildings were designed for a campus setting and landscaping gave the researcher the feeling of being at the academy, not in industry. Tenants in Stanford Industrial Park were allowed access to campus laboratory facilities and the land leases generated money to finance the growth of the university. Varian Associates and Hewlett-Packard, both started by Stanford alums, were the first two companies to lease space in the highly successful 660-acre industrial park. It became a bridge of collaboration between the academy and business which generated brain-power for

the research firms and supported university coffers. Stanford Industrial Park acted as a generator for start-up electronics firms where eleven thousand workers were employed in twenty-five companies by 1961. Its landscaping, architecture and physical layout became the model for subsequent research and development facilities which portrayed a modern, innovative image.[25]

Lockheed, a Van Nuys, California-based aircraft corporation had grown during World War II, and the Cold War stimulated more defense department contracts. The company was named for Allan and Malcolm Loughead, brothers who lived part of their childhood in the Santa Clara Valley and later pioneered in aircraft construction when they built their own hydroplanes. The Loughead brothers first achieved fame when they thrilled hundreds of tourists with hydroplane rides for $10 at the Panama Pacific Exposition in San Francisco in 1915. So it was an interesting twist of history that the Southern California Corporation, descended from the brothers' hydroplane business, purchased 275 acres of land near Sunnyvale in 1955, only a short distance from the childhood home of the Lougheads in Santa Clara County.

Lockheed operated out of Stanford Industrial Park from its arrival in the Bay Area in 1954 when a new wing of the company was formed called Lockheed Missile Systems Division and moved to new buildings in Sunnyvale in 1956. The company chose Sunnyvale on the recommendation of one of the new division's directors, Herschel Brown. It was hoped the Sunnyvale property would provide easy access to recent college graduates, "an agreeable climate, a good quality of living, affordability and proximity to an airport."[26]

Marion Sellers, by 1990 a forty-year veteran at Lockheed, actually orchestrated the move from Van Nuys to Sunnyvale in 1956. He recalled that Labor Day weekend when six hundred people formed a caravan of 350 moving vans and traveled from the Los Angeles area to the north. Over the following six weeks, two thousand co-workers joined the initial transferees. Ground-breaking at the new Sunnyvale site took place in what Sellers recalled "was all beanfields then, and the Bayshore Freeway was only a two-lane road."

In the late 1950s, the Missiles and Space Division concentrated its efforts on developing ballistic missiles, particularly those that could be launched from shipdeck at sea and from submarines. Dubbed Polaris, after the North Star, the early series of missiles were deployed by July of 1960, when they were launched from the submerged nuclear submarine the USS *George Washington*.

The space race began in earnest in 1961 when the Russians successfully launched *Vostok I*, carrying the first man into space. The Space Systems Division of Lockheed produced the Agena, an upper stage rocket used for launch vehicles Atlas, Titan and Thor. Later, the Agena was critical in the Gemini program for space rendezvous and docking purposes. Near the Lockheed plant in Sunnyvale, the National Aeronautics and Space Act of July 29, 1958 transferred all assets and functions of NACA to NASA and research continued at Ames Laboratory. Projects during the 1950s and 1960s included hypervelocity free-flight experiments, airflow studies, pilot-environment adaptation research, aerodynamic heating, space physics, and flight simulators.[27]

Like Lockheed, General Motors also intended to build a new facility in Northern California. Southern Pacific Railroad wanted to sell the land to GM. A vice-president from Southern Pacific's real estate division contacted Sunnyvale Chamber Manager Al Spiers asking for all pertinent information on Sunnyvale and specifically on Oakmead Ranch at Bayshore Highway and Lawrence Station Road. The ranch, a former horse-breeding farm, had a three-story farm house, a windmill, a few barns and several out-building shacks. Migrant families lived on the ranch and paid $15 per month for their families to live in dilapidated cabins. They were very disappointed, however, when they were told they would have to move to make way for the giant car production plant.

The ranch was owned by a man named Paul Cohn and it had been annexed by Sunnyvale and zoned for industrial use. Cohn attempted to have the zoning restric-

tions changed so that he could sell his property to a residential real estate developer for housing tracts. After two failed attempts to rezone for residential, Cohn sold to Southern Pacific for $3,750 per acre.

Ultimately, General Motors bought the two-hundred acres from Southern Pacific. The chamber of commerce and Sunnyvale City Council were ecstatic over their latest coup in drawing a major industrial client to Sunnyvale. General Motors' President Harlow Curtice said Sunnyvale's industrial zoning was the main factor that swayed him to locate the plant in Sunnyvale. Some citizens were worried that a General Motors plant would create a smog problem, however, City Manager Hunter assured them that "we have strict performance standards: no odors, no fumes, or other nuisances. We haven't got a factory smokestack in the city." He promised residents that a General Motors plant would not be a polluter.[28]

The two hundred acres, however, were the subject of a boundary dispute between the cities of Sunnyvale and Santa Clara. It is unclear whether this dispute alone or in combination with other factors contributed to General Motors' decision to locate in Fremont three years later. The value of the land GM bought in Sunnyvale from Southern Pacific Railroad increased from almost $4,000 to $12,000 an acre from the time of purchase to the time of decision to locate in Fremont. General Motors exchanged the property in Sunnyvale with other property owned by Southern Pacific in Fremont and SP got its valuable land back for future development. Ten years went by, however, before Southern Pacific developed Oakmead Business and Industrial Park on the "GM site" which straddles the boundary between Santa Clara and Sunnyvale. It was almost by chance then, that an auto plant was not built at what today is Highway 101 and the Lawrence Expressway. Sunnyvale officials desperately wanted General Motors in their town and were sorely disappointed when the company chose to build in Fremont.

It was a time of municipal imperialism in Santa Clara County and a look at literature generated by the chamber of commerce in Sunnyvale shows an egotistical attitude common to many towns in that era. The chamber, capitalizing on Walter Crossman's promotional "City of Destiny," felt that Sunnyvale was "destined" for great things. A pamphlet entitled "The City With the Built-in Future" bursts with the rhetoric of growth:

> Industrially and residentially, I am a thoroughly
> thought-out, well-planned, near-perfect Community.
> When I was but a sprawling, gangling, crossroad on
> the California map, my City-planning Commission
> and a professional planning consultant worked with
> the thorough cooperation of my Chamber of Commerce
> to make plans for my future. They neatly divided my
> acreage into an industrial-residential planned type
> zoning, with a portion of my land specifically set aside
> for improved industrial use . . . . As a direct result of
> their astute activity then, my industrial area today has
> paved streets, adequate sewerage, plenty of water, a
> practically inexhaustible supply of natural gas, and
> one of the country's most powerful electric supply
> lines at hand.[29]

There is no reference to the property owners of the rezoned areas, nor is there an indication that land for new streets had been taken from some unwilling farmers. A 1954 chamber of commerce annual report entitled "Growing Without Pain" optimistically overlooked many constituents whose farms were carved into unusable pieces.

Ruel Charles Olson was one of these farmers who fought the city's attempts to claim a portion of his cherry orchard to widen and lengthen Fair Oaks Avenue between Old San Francisco Road and El Camino Real. He formed the "Fair Oaks Citizens Committee," but it was unsuccessful in stopping the bulldozers which uprooted his trees and Olson was assessed $17,000 for "improvements" to his land.[30]

Impending change that had been almost imperceptible at the beginning of the decade was completely undeniable in later years. It was as if Sunnyvale were trying to make everything new and replace the old. The population

boom resulted in new neighborhoods, schools, shopping centers and a supporting infrastructure of streets and utilities which were built at phenomenal rates.

In 1953, Sunnyvale installed 328 parking meters, its first, acknowledging the impact of traffic in the town. Twenty-three churches were under construction by 1957, some replacing older, smaller ones, and others, brand new. By 1958 Sunnyvale boasted that its thirty-three-member volunteer civic improvement committee "crushed public

Ruel Charles Olson and Rose (Zamar) Olson standing near their cherry stand, circa 1940. Courtesy California History Center, Stocklmeir Library/Archives, Michelle Ann Jacobson Collection.

complacency" to promote a $6,800,000 bond issue for improvements to highways, sewer system, purchase of new park lands, five fire stations, and construction of a new civic center.[31]

Sunnyvale Plaza Shopping Center was built in the 1950s tradition of Main Street U.S.A., where townspeople would venture for retail shopping, banking and other business. Sunnyvale Plaza's major tenants were Hart's Department Store, J. C. Penney, J. J. Newberry, Weinstein's and Woolworth's. Constructed in the heart of downtown Sunnyvale, they virtually severed all retail ties with San José which had been the urban center for the agricultural communities of the Santa Clara Valley. Up to this time, county services, major retailers, and cultural events were all located in San José and the rail link from San Francisco to San José served all the towns between, taking Sunnyvaleans to San José's downtown. The development of stronger city government and the building of local shopping centers dealt a fatal blow to the link between Sunnyvale and San José and the growing city had very little need for connection with San José. A similar phenomenon occurred in other Santa Clara Valley towns, contributing to the atrophy of downtown San José.

There was a short-lived trend in California cities and towns in the 1950s to purchase land in outlying areas for parks and recreational use by their citizens. Sunnyvale purchased 250 acres in the Santa Cruz Mountains for $50,000. The park, located almost five miles south of Saratoga Gap on Skyline Boulevard, offered camping, hiking and picnics for Sunnyvale residents only.[32] Fifteen years later the city sold the park to the county to generate cash for municipal projects.

One symbol of Sunnyvale's historic past was the rapidly deteriorating Martin Murphy, Jr. twenty-room house

Sunnyvale Plaza on Taaffe Street under construction in the 1950s. Chamber of Commerce Manager Al Spiers (on right) is pictured with Plaza developers. Courtesy Sunnyvale Historical Society & Museum Association.

Post card of Plaza Shopping Center, circa 1950s. Courtesy Ann Zarko.

which the city had purchased in 1951 in order to establish a park and monument. Some advocated demolishing the rundown house, while others mobilized to convince the city to save the irreplaceable building. A small group of preservation-minded residents met toward the end of 1956 and drew up articles of incorporation to form the Sunnyvale Historical Society. Their main goal was to save the Murphy house and they began by boarding up windows to discourage vandalism and securing a caretaker for the property. They also successfully got the house named a state historic landmark, eligible for restoration funds from the state. "Progress" prevailed, however, when the historical society did not have enough clout to convince their own city leaders to invest dollars to save the hundred-year-old home and the building was bulldozed in 1961. Despite its defeat, the Sunnyvale Historical Society continued to meet and established a museum, collecting thousands of artifacts and photographs, creating programs for school children and preserving other historic buildings and trees in town.

Murphy house demolition in 1961. Courtesy Sunnyvale Historical Society & Museum Association.

Public auction held at old Murphy house before it was razed in 1961. Courtesy Sunnyvale Historical Society & Museum Association.

In 1958, City Manager Hunter resigned and handed the reigns over to Perry Scott who was hired by the city council, and at the same time an amendment was made to the city charter calling for seven council members instead of five. Both city managers, the city council and the chamber of commerce were exceedingly proud of the transformation that occurred in Sunnyvale from the end of World War II to 1960. They had molded the agricultural town into an industrial city capitalizing on the population increases resulting from the War. The Sunnyvale of just under 10,000 residents of 1950 had grown to a city of 53,000 by 1960.

Chapter 6

SUNNYVALE'S SCHIZOPHRENIA

By 1960 Sunnyvale residents, businesses and political leaders began to feel repercussions from the unrestrained growth of the 1950s and there was no indication it would stop. The last traffic light on the Bayshore Highway between San Francisco and San José was removed at Fair Oaks Avenue, and Central Expressway was built as streets were widened and extended, taking valuable portions of farms, rendering them useless for large scale fruit production. Some orchardists wanted to hold out against the developers while other farmers or their sons became real estate developers themselves, promoting and profiting from change. The canning industry went through its own painful transition because of fewer orchards supplying their operations, and California Canners and Growers (CAL CAN) acquired Schuckl & Company in 1963.

Rezoning battles followed in the wake of annexations and street building. The Vidovich family, for example, Sunnyvale farmers for more than a generation, submitted a request to the county in 1963 to rezone their farm land at Mary and Fremont avenues for commercial use. Although outside Sunnyvale city limits, Mary Avenue had recently been extended, and bisected the Vidovich farm. Ironically, even city officials who had aggressively annexed other properties to Sunnyvale, opposed the request for rezoning this land, as did residents and neighboring property owners. Steve Vidovich stated the family's point of view when he explained:

We would have been perfectly happy to have continued farming the area, but this 86 foot wide Mary Avenue extension will divide our farm in half. It kills the land's usefulness for farming.[1]

Ultimately the Vidovich family's request for rezoning was granted by the county board of supervisors. The press claimed the board members were "disdaining the vociferous pleas of some 100 Sunnyvale citizens."[2] The city limits subsequently were extended well past the area, and De Anza Square Shopping Center was built on nine acres there.

Likewise, Remington Avenue was extended and the Pavlina family, who had been growing cherries and apricots since the 1920s, decided to develop their forty-plus acres themselves. Peter Pavlina built the Remington Grove Apartments, a medical building, and in the early 1970s he built Pavlina Plaza Shopping Center on El Camino Real. The city built the community center on some of their land. Pavlina at one time served as president of Sunnyvale's Chamber of Commerce.[3]

Orchardists struggled to formulate their own reaction to growth. For many, leaving the farm meant abandoning a way of life that they loved. For others, the cash generated by the sale and development of land was a welcome relief, providing a secure economic future. Ruel Olson, who had unsuccessfully opposed the widening of Fair Oaks Avenue, attempted to maintain a grip on his family property and way of life by fighting annexation and

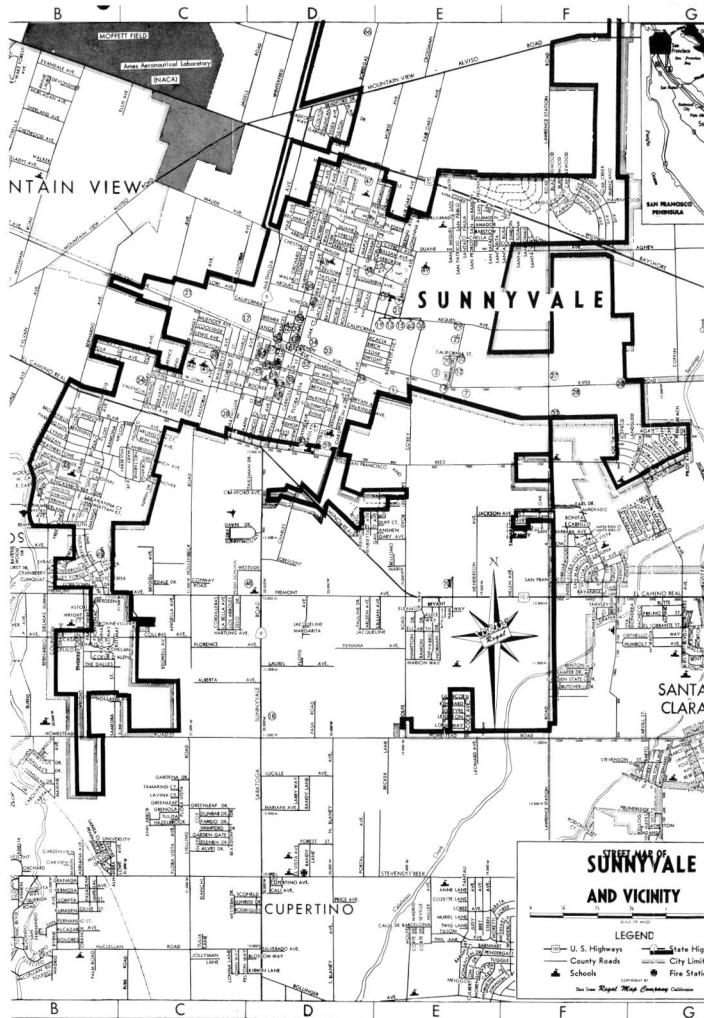

Map of Sunnyvale, circa 1955. Note the irregular boundaries as properties were annexed and the pockets of land remaining outside the incorporated area. Courtesy Sunnyvale Public Library.

and-a-half acres in the middle of his orchard were plowed under to make way for the six-lane Mathilda Avenue.[4]

Other counties in the state were also experiencing the rapid elimination of agricultural land. In 1965 the state legislature, under pressure from Santa Clara County farmers among others, passed the Williamson Act which stipulated that actively farmed land would be taxed on the profit of the crops, not the value of the land. If farmers protected their farms under the Williamson Act, they had to agree to farm for ten years or have their property reassessed at commercial rates. The Williamson Act was one of the few successful agricultural conservation laws. It was supported by Karl Belser, a Santa Clara County planning director during the 1950s and 1960s, who was highly critical of the elimination of agriculture from the valley and of annexation proceedings by San José and other towns. Belser had few political allies, however, and his attempts to save agriculture in Santa Clara County were largely unsuccessful.

Massive infrastructure development by the city, the county, and the state continued despite some farmers' desire to hold on to their property. Sunnyvale's population had quadrupled in the 1950s so that in 1960 the city had 53,000 residents. By 1970 there were 95,408 Sunnyvaleans. The Public Works Department added 92 miles of streets in the 1960s, for a total of 233 miles. Major projects included Kifer Road, Arques, Fremont Avenue, Wolfe Road, and the Moffett Industrial Park roads of Crossman, Caribbean, Java Drive and the Mathilda Avenue extension. Santa Clara County purchased land from homeowners to build the Central and Lawrence expressways. The state made progress on Highway 280, the Stevens Creek Freeway (Hwy. 85), Mountain View/Alviso Highway (Hwy. 237), and the Bayshore Freeway (Hwy. 101).[5]

By the mid-1960s, Sunnyvale had twenty elementary schools, three intermediate schools and five high schools educating over 20,000 students. The number of schools and pupils illustrates the explosive growth of the town-turning-city.[6]

The construction boom of the 1950s had successfully

eminent domain proceedings. His cherry orchard bordered El Camino Real and the city wanted to extend Mathilda Avenue to enable Lockheed workers to commute across town. Still angered by the Fair Oaks extension, Olson fought the city to protect his orchards. He was accused of thwarting progress and ultimately lost his five-year battle when two-

alleviated fears of unemployment in the immediate postwar years. However new and unforeseen problems arose out of the scramble to build and develop. The pace of development was faster than local governments could monitor, and the lack of general policy toward growth resulted in power struggles between and within governmental structures at the regional, county, and municipal level.

As the boom continued into the 1960s, Sunnyvale suffered numerous internal conflicts resulting in civic disruption and political shuffling. By the end of the decade, Sunnyvale had seen eight mayors and four city managers while incumbent councilmembers played musical chairs with recently elected representatives. To a large extent, the proponents of the "new order" established in 1949 with the adoption of the city charter were booted out while political leaders jockeyed for power and attempted to adjust to the changes.

A shift in policy and power in Sunnyvale began in 1963 when the formerly popular chamber of commerce manager Al Spiers was fired by the chamber's board. Although he had been credited with bringing some of the biggest employers to Sunnyvale he was told that he was not keeping up with the times. Sunnyvale had changed, and as one board member said, they were ready for "a flannel trouser operator," a professional marketing specialist. Spiers was accused of lacking administrative skills because there was high turnover in his chamber staff. Interestingly, Spiers was personally popular and had a very loyal following of local citizens who lobbied the chamber to keep him on the job. It is ironic, and perhaps exemplifies the mood in town, that one of the most vocal catalysts for change in Sunnyvale in the 1950s was accused of not changing enough in the 1960s.

Spiers was subsequently hired by Cupertino as chamber manager, but within two years retired because of ill health. He remained living in Sunnyvale even after he was fired, continued to be active in the community and was named Cupertino's "Man of the Year" in 1969 in recognition of his community service. In 1963 the Sunnyvale Chamber

of Commerce hired Ed Beaty of Stockton to replace Spiers.

Civic tumult began for the city council and manager the same year when in a heated debate in council chambers, real estate man and former Planning Commissioner Don Koreski was appointed to the city council seat left vacant by Mark Russell's resignation. Councilwoman Maureen McDaniel, though unsuccessful, opposed his appointment because she did not want anyone associated with the real estate business on the council. The following year, City Manager Perry Scott fired seven-year Planning Director Arthur Spencer after property secretly owned by two planning commissioners at the corner of Reedland and Timber Pine avenues was rezoned by the city council. Spencer protested his dismissal because he and his staff recommended against rezoning the land. The two commissioners, John Houlihan and Donald S. Logan, denied that their ownership was secret even though their names did not appear on the application for rezoning.[7] This battle just barely preceeded an all-out war that was heating up over the city manager's job.

In 1964, former Finance Department Director Thomas H. Sweeney was appointed acting city manager to replace Perry Scott and was granted permanent appointment the next year. He was only the third city manager in Sunnyvale's history, but the first one to come from a city hall job. Amid rumors of personality conflicts between Sweeney and his subordinates, Sweeney requested the resignation of two department heads, the City Librarian Colin Lucas and longtime Parks and Recreation Director Richard Milkovich. The requests touched off a months-long civic furor with citizen groups forming on one side and the city council attempting to maintain order on the other.[8] Fearing a walk-out by the whole city staff, the city council voted to suspend Sweeney. His only official ally was Councilwoman Maureen McDaniel.

Director of Community Relations Gordon Miller was named interim city manager. He had been one of the five threatening to quit if Milkovich was not reinstated. His first act was to rehire Milkovich, and by then, Sweeney requested that his case have a public hearing. In the meantime, public support for Sweeney grew. Over one hundred supporters including a few prominent local real estate developers launched a door-to-door campaign to collect signatures on a petition asking for a fair and impartial hearing for Sweeney. Some believed the city council had it in for Sweeney. One supporter declared, "If a group of employees can gang up on Mr. Sweeney, we don't have a city manager form of government." Right up to the public hearing in February 1967 when he resigned, Sweeney maintained that he knew "no cause to justify this action [his suspension]."

A record twenty-two candidates filed applications to run for city council that year. The debate over the power of the city manager might have influenced people to run but the April election did not effect much change. Five of seven members were reelected, including Sweeney supporter Maureen McDaniel. Former City Planning Commissioner Donald Logan, the same who submitted an application to rezone a piece of property under another name, unseated Fred Logan (no relation).

All this time, while local government was embroiled in conflict and accusation, a new phenomenon was silently emerging on a national level and having major impact on a distracted Sunnyvale. The "military-industrial complex," a term coined by President Dwight Eisenhower referring to the economic power of the network of defense contractors, was growing to gigantic proportions, even within Sunnyvale's own city limits. Eisenhower had cautioned, "In the councils of government, we must guard against the acquisition of unwarranted influence, whether sought or unsought, by the military-industrial complex."[9] His concern about the growing economic power from Pentagon projects proved legitimate because by the end of the decade, the military-industrial complex was an $80 billion-a-year industry which completely dominated Sunnyvale's economy.

While a local military presence was obvious because of Moffett Field, other more secretive operations emerged as well. In 1960, the top-secret Sunnyvale Air Force Station

(later renamed Onizuka Air Force Base) was established near Lockheed's facilities. The Cold War fueled the projects at this little-known Sunnyvale base.

Trends in Sunnyvale's industries reflected those in other areas in the United States where the defense industry was the basis for the economy. Historian Charles Wollenberg noted in Golden Gate Metropolis that

> whereas 19th and 20th century industrial development needed to locate close to markets, resources, and transportation routes, the new high-tech enterprises stimulated by defense dollars put a premium on easy access to appropriate brainpower and technical skills.[10]

Military spending had a major impact on local and regional planning policies where defense industries created "low density, industrial park suburbs" disconnected from nearby urban areas like San José and San Francisco. The result was a "newer generation of medium-sized, detached metropolitan areas,"[11] precisely what Sunnyvale and the Santa Clara Valley were becoming.

In the wake of the Korean War, the Cold War and the climate of accelerated military buildup, the principal products produced in Sunnyvale were spy satellites, missiles, radar equipment based on the Hansen/Varian brothers' invention of the Klystron tube, and microwave detection/ communication systems. Virtually all were produced for contracts with the defense department or NASA. By 1966 seventy percent of industry sales in the valley was the result of government spending.[12]

Buildings began to sprout up on former farms to house defense contractors and their associated industries. A worldwide construction and engineering firm, the Guy F. Atkinson Company, bought six hundred acres from fifteen property owners in Sunnyvale in 1963 and formed Moffett Industrial Park. Their plan called for an industrial park specifically geared to science and electronics companies that supplied the defense department along with their distribution centers. The $7 million transaction, the largest real

Air Force Station Sunnyvale, subsequently dubbed the "Blue Cube" and eventually renamed Onizuka Air Force Base. Courtesy City of Sunnyvale.

estate deal to date in the county, resulted in a new industrial park that was expected to be filled to capacity within five to eight years and employ ten to twenty thousand workers.

The fifteen property sellers were granted short term leasebacks on the land until the end of the growing season to harvest crops already planted. Meanwhile the city annexed those parcels not already within the city limits in order to capitalize on a broader tax base. Moffett Industrial Park was modeled on Stanford Industrial Park and became the largest master-planned development for high-technology industry

Early stages of development of Moffett Industrial Park. Note the street was named for the original town promoter, "Crossman." Courtesy Sunnyvale Historical Society & Museum Association.

in the nation.

After the assassination of President John Kennedy, America's participation in the war in Southeast Asia rapidly escalated and national participation was justified in the name of eradicating the spread of communism. The war in Vietnam had direct economic impact in Sunnyvale because of the preponderance of defense contractors. In a Newsweek article, reporter Peter Barnes was surprised at the invisibility of weapons production in Sunnyvale:

> In its physical appearance, Sunnyvale has turned into another dreary stretch of urban America, its orchards replaced by shopping centers, bowling alleys, used-car lots, and drive-ins. Strangely enough, the omnipres-ent industrial complex is almost invisible . . . . Missiles and rockets are put together in bland, sanitized buildings almost indistinguishable from cafeterias and insurance company offices. No signs proclaim the change from "prune capital" to "Polaris capital of the world."[13]

Mayor Harold Shields, a contracts administrator for

Westinghouse, explained that workers in Sunnyvale defense plants did not think of themselves as builders of war ma-chines, since the Poseidon and Polaris missiles were offen-sive weapons and therefore deterrents. Shields claimed that the Poseidon and Polaris "are never intended to be used."[14]

An unidentified Santa Clara County planner was quoted as saying "Death is our favorite industry." Other officials preferred more diplomatic language and denied that an end to the war in Vietnam would send Sunnyvale's economy into a tailspin. Mayor Shields asserted that peace would bring war dollars back home for long-term military research and development. International arms control, however, was viewed as a threat to the area's economy. Senior county planner Robert Goldman said "a really meaningful [international arms] agreement could put our Lockheed plant essentially out of business." He concluded, however, that such an agreement was "in the realm of fantasy."[15]

While Sunnyvale's complete dependence on military procurement did not produce a widespread pro-war atti-tude, neither was it a hotbed of dissent. Interestingly, the largest labor union representing Lockheed workers, District 508 of the International Association of Machinists, officially opposed the war in Vietnam, but did not require members to hold the same view.

The Vietnam War also had a personal impact for many residents whose sons or daughters went to Vietnam. In 1965, Sunnyvale resident Marine Sergeant R. L. Jones was awarded the Bronze Star by Congress for valor in his service in Vietnam. The citation made specific reference to Jones' "disregard for his own personal safety [as] he repeatedly exposed himself to intense hostile fire while carrying wounded men to safety."[16] Despite the heavy influence of defense work in Sunnyvale, there is no evidence that Viet-nam veterans were greeted with more than perfunctory acknowledgment on their return home.

Toward the end of the decade the Atkinson Com-pany formed a partnership with Prudential Insurance Company and Lockheed Missiles & Space Company as

Moffett Park Associates to manage the project where one advertisement proclaimed, "Plants Grow Beautifully in Moffett Park." Companies could build on sites as small as two acres and count on future expansion on adjoining acreage. Expectations of full occupancy within five to eight years proved unrealistic, however, as by 1970 there were only three tenants, all defense-related companies: Lockheed Missiles & Space, Electro-Magnetic Systems Laboratories (ESL), and Control Data Corporation. In 1972, Prudential bought out the other partners on fifty-three acres in the industrial park, with an option to control the remaining 417 acres, which they exercised throughout the 1970s.[17]

Sunnyvale's Chamber of Commerce and City Council, like most everyone else, viewed the emerging high-technology centers as clean, innovative and entrepreneurial, an improvement over the smoke-belching, bureaucratic, conservative industries in the East. Lockheed Missiles & Space Company's expansion, Ford Aerospace and ESL were welcomed with open arms to Sunnyvale just as Westinghouse had been the decade before.

Even though defense-related companies grew up in Sunnyvale, they had almost no political or cultural ties to the community. They created their own reclusive environment with strict security measures, aimed at keeping information in and those lacking security clearance out. Access to educated managers and a general work force with proximity to the military base at Moffett were more important than what particular city would be listed as the company address.

By 1969 Lockheed Missiles & Space Company employed 21,000 workers in the design and production of Polaris and Poseidon missiles and the Agena rocket. Westinghouse in Sunnyvale employed 3,000 to design and build missile launch tubes for Polaris, Poseidon and Trident submarines. The 1,400 workers at United Technology Center produced rocket boosters for missile systems while thousands of others worked for businesses dependent on the giant defense contractors.

Civic leaders had been successful in decreasing Sunnyvale's economic dependence on the fruit industry.

Ironically, total economic dependence rested not only on one industry, but on one customer: the federal government. Attempts to create a broad-based diversified economy had failed, and this was in part because no provision had been made for continued farming in Sunnyvale and Santa Clara County.

The semiconductor industry in Santa Clara County developed in symbiosis with the military-industrial complex according to Jack Melchor, a founding investor of Electro-Magnetic Systems Laboratories (ESL). He claimed that defense contracts caused an acceleration in the semiconductor business and that "the U.S. government, through big defense systems programs, really built the semiconductor industry, because they were crying for solid-state devices and high reliability."[18] The military-industrial complex and the semiconductor industries evolved together and naturally located near each other to supply each other's needs and feed off each other. Bay Area college campuses along with Moffett Field offered a steady stream of workers. Scores of subcontractors likewise located near the industrial vortex and the emergence of Moffett Industrial Park on property

Lockheed building 940 in Sunnyvale. Courtesy City of Sunnyvale.

adjacent to Lockheed and Moffett Field established an environment ripe for defense-based industrial development.

New technologies, which up to this point were accessible only to specialized companies, began to encourage broader-based applications. In 1965, a patent attorney for Lockheed, twenty-nine-year-old Jack L. Bohan, set up Sunnyvale's patent library to allow easier access for patent searches. One of only thirty-three in the nation, it was the only one outside of Washington, D. C. also classified by subject, facilitating very thorough patent searches. The Patent Information Clearinghouse (PIC) was instrumental in securing numerous patents issued for high-tech inventions by local entrepreneurs and engineers in Silicon Valley, and today makes millions of patents accessible. The PIC can produce copies of every patent ever issued by the U. S. Patent Office, either from microfilm or CD-ROM (computer disk), beginning with Patent Number 1, issued to George Washington in 1790 for his personal formula for making potash. Presently the PIC produces a positive cash flow for the City of Sunnyvale, and it remains a resource unmatched in most other major cities.

While new industrial development flourished on the north side of the Bayshore Freeway and in new industrial parks, the old downtown of Sunnyvale was deteriorating rapidly. Several proposals were put forth as possible solutions to the decline in retail sales at Sunnyvale Plaza and local shops because Sunnyvale residents also shopped at outlying centers such as Mayfield Mall, San Antonio Shopping Center, and Valley Fair.

Since federal urban renewal dollars were made available to blighted residential areas of cities in the 1960s, Sunnyvale applied for federal monies to remove existing buildings and redevelop the land now occupied by Town & Country Village. Hoping to bolster sales at Sunnyvale Plaza, the city petitioned the federal government for funds to clear and redevelop thirty-two acres of land occupied by dilapidated residential and commercial buildings bounded by Mathilda Avenue to the west, Evelyn to the north, Murphy Avenue to the east and Washington to the south. Rundown

houses and shacks on Briggs Street as well as Frances and Taaffe would be bulldozed for redevelopment as well as the commercial buildings on the 100 block of Murphy Avenue. Federal requirements to qualify for funds stated that the bulk of the blighted property had to be residential so the 100 block of Murphy Avenue, which today is the city's only historic district, was disallowed as part of the urban renewal program because it was a commercial street. If the federal government had not enforced this stipulation, the present-day historic district would not exist because city officials wanted the Murphy Avenue block razed. The remaining nineteen acres were rezoned commercial, and developed under the guise of the "Encina Urban Renewal Plan." Among the buildings demolished was the *Sociedad Cervantes Española* headquarters which had been completed barely fifteen years earlier at a cost of $96,000. Parking and streets were provided by the city, and Town & Country Village Inc. bought the remaining land for $285,000 on June 21, 1966. Town & Country Village, a 65,000-square-foot open mall of sixty stores adjacent to Sunnyvale Plaza opened in 1968.

Dollars spent on construction hit an all-time high in 1968, with $54.3 million spent on a combination of residential, commercial, and industrial properties. In 1969, 420 residential building permits were issued for construction valued at $9,990,635, while industrial building permits represented $9,582,072. Shopping centers sprouted all over Sunnyvale in the 1960s. In addition to the ten-year old Sunnyvale Plaza on Taaffe Street, the Hacienda Shopping Center, the new Town & Country Village, and Westmoor Village opened while retail strip centers blossomed on El Camino, Mathilda and Fair Oaks avenues.

Along with the deteriorating downtown, old city hall at Murphy and McKinley avenues had fallen into disrepair since it was vacated for the new civic center a few blocks away. From the time it was built in 1929, the mission-style building with a red tile roof had been a social as well as political center where the large auditorium and stage hosted city council meetings, dramatic presentations, social gatherings and holiday festivities. During canning season in the

1930s and 1940s, it was the scene of popular Saturday night dances. Many Sunnyvale residents favored renovation of the old building which was offered for sale at $200,000 and subsequently reduced to $150,000. The citizens' group that favored preservation of the site could not raise the funds to buy the property and the city refused to spend money to renovate it.

The venerable old building became a scapegoat as merchants blamed its vacant presence for sluggish retail sales and demanded its removal. Downtown shopkeepers felt that if the site were sold and developed into retail-commercial businesses, their own shops would prosper. Joe Battaglia of Ferry's Hardware Store voiced the merchants' opinion when he said, "the property is just sitting idle there. If we could put in some nice stores, the city would get more revenue and we could keep people shopping in downtown Sunnyvale."[19] The merchants demanded that the city sell the old city hall.

At several city council meetings, demolition of city hall was a hotly contested agenda item as many citizens pleaded with council members to preserve the building. However, no one protested at the final meeting on the issue when the council called for demolition bids. The press noted the formidable presence of former City Clerk Ida Trubschenck who had been a force in Sunnyvale government long before the city hall was built. Miss Trubschenck sat in the last row and remained silent throughout the entire meeting.[20]

In the view of the town merchants, the razing of city hall came several years too late, but those who favored preservation felt the city should have saved the historic property. As if to soothe the gaping wound left by demolition, the city later agreed to save the redwood and cypress trees surrounding the site and incorporate them into future redevelopment, but only after Fern Ohrt, an elderly townswoman threatened to stand in front of the bulldozers if they attempted to destroy the trees.

Somewhat remorseful over the destruction of the old Murphy homestead a few years earlier, the city bought seven

Ida Trubschenck, a formidable presence in Sunnyvale city government from the town's incorporation through the 1960s. Miss Trubschenck was city clerk and many of her handwritten records survive in the collection at Sunnyvale Public Library. Courtesy Sunnyvale Historical Society & Museum Association.

lots at California and Sunnyvale avenues, where the Murphy family's Bay View house had been. Unbelievably, the city looked to the state and federal government for a historic sites grant, even though they had already demolished the former Murphy house, the very thing that made the site historic. The land was turned into Murphy Park and a concrete block recreation building replaced the irreplaceable first frame house in Santa Clara County.

Construction of Murphy Park, site of the former Murphy house, 1960s. Courtesy Sunnyvale Historical Society & Museum Association.

The identity of the town changed dramatically. The title of the <u>Newsweek</u> article, "Sunnyvale: Prunes to Missiles," and Newell Industries' advertisement "From Apricots to Megahertz" aptly described the identity crisis facing the city. It was as if Sunnyvale suffered from a schizophrenia in the 1960s. On the one hand, local downtown merchants lobbied for redevelopment, urban renewal and razing old city hall. They envisioned that their turf would remain the social and political focal point of the city. At the same time, however, larger entities such as the defense department and large-scale real estate developers were gaining a strong economic foothold in Sunnyvale. As defense-related employment rose, land was purchased and developed into industrial parks whose owners and tenants had little or no interest in the economic health of downtown. Each of these diverging constituencies felt that they held the key to the city's future. This split personality led directly to an attempt in the 1970s to reclaim lost identity by replacing the old downtown with a centralized, regional shopping mall.

Chapter 7

"Heart Transplant"

In 1971, Electronic News editor Don C. Hoefler wrote a series of three articles entitled "Silicon Valley—U.S.A." which nicknamed Santa Clara County where the evolution of the semiconductor had occurred. He outlined a genealogy of companies that evolved, one from another, after eight engineers "defected" from Shockley Transistor Corporation in 1957 to form Fairchild Semiconductor. Hoefler's articles virtually renamed the county, the appellation stuck, and the world has come to know the county more as "Silicon Valley" than by the actual names of cities and towns in the region.

Shockley Transistor Corporation was "the direct antecedent of nearly every semiconductor firm in the area . . . ." according to Hoefler.[1] Robert Noyce, one of the "traitorous eight" who left the company, headed Fairchild Semiconductor until 1968 when he started microchip manufacturer Intel Corporation. In 1969, Advanced Micro Devices was founded by eight former employees of Fairchild. Between 1959 and 1979, more than fifty separate companies were founded by former Fairchild employees.

The microprocessor was introduced in 1971 by Intel Corporation and in 1976 Sunnyvale native Steve Wozniak built a home computer from a used microprocessor he bought for $20. Wozniak joined forces with another young computer wizard, Steve Jobs, to form Apple Computer which introduced the personal computer in 1977. Allied businesses sprouted in the technologically fertile valley and electronics products replaced the bounty of orchards and vineyards.

Silicon Valley flourished partly because of a new method of amassing capital to finance business ventures. Companies no longer relied solely on banks for business loans but on venture capitalists willing to take risks by investing large amounts of cash in start-up companies. They based their investment on business plans and to some extent, hunches. The venture capital companies supported the technologists' need for cash and the available cash flow encouraged new generations of high-technology firms. In the tradition of electronics giants Hewlett-Packard and Varian, fledgling entrepreneurs started new businesses in garages and at kitchen tables in Silicon Valley at an incredible rate. In response to this phenomenon, real estate developers built and leased "incubator" spaces like Fair Oaks Business Park in Sunnyvale. Built in the 1970s, it housed thirty-five "garage enterprises" and was a springboard to success for some tenants. In one such venture, a group of former Hewlett-Packard employees formed TRIUS, and opened their business in Fair Oaks Business Park. Partner Bill Ballenbach said, "you get into the entrepreneur thing with the idea of becoming the master of your own destiny."[2] Hundreds of Silicon Valley marketing specialists and engineers left secure, well-paid jobs to strike out on their own and form new companies.

Major success stories in the Silicon Valley "gold rush" were as relatively short-lived as the first California gold rush in 1849. Ultimately there were many more failures than successful ventures, but throughout the 1970s and into the 1980s, the mentality of the valley maintained the image of a garage tinkerer suddenly turned affluent chief executive officer. Moira Johnston, in a 1982 article for National Geographic, decribed the Silicon Valley as:

> an incestuous network of suppliers, customers, venture capitalists, brains, research institutes, computer and software companies, schools, and headhunters, the executive recruiters who move men around the valley at a dizzying rate in a tradition of musical jobs that is a key to the valley's contagious vitality.[3]

She also noted, however, that the success stories did not apply to all as evidenced by over 120,000 assembly-line workers of various ethnic backgrounds who could not afford to buy homes in the valley.

Although Moffett Industrial Park was Silicon Valley's largest industrial development in the early 1970s, it was by no means the only one. Real estate speculation on industrial land and buildings erupted on a very large scale in Sunnyvale in response to Moffett Park's track record and the growing high-technology production in all of Silicon Valley. Just as the revolution in semiconductors relied upon venture capitalists as an alternative to traditional bank financing, so the availability of the venture capital money produced a whole group of real estate speculators. They built industrial parks "on spec," gambling that the high-technology revolution would generate demand for the buildings that sprouted on former farm land throughout Sunnyvale. The developers themselves, and eventually the real estate agents working for them, marketed the buildings and drew the companies to Sunnyvale. Ultimately they took over the role of civic booster that the chamber of commerce had traditionally played. The chamber was no longer the only marketing agent for the city because the real estate business did it for them. City Manager John E. Dever articulated the differences from the 1950s process of encour-

aging industrial growth:

> Years ago, the city encouraged development to industrial firms by extending services and a national advertising campaign. Now it's moved to the stage where we call on developers, rather than the businesses.[4]

In 1973, Dever announced that forty-three buildings totaling 890,000 square feet were under construction in Sunnyvale, to bring the total to 193 industrial buildings. Sixty electronics firms were in Sunnyvale that year.

Nogales Industrial Park, off Mathilda Avenue near Maude and second in size to Moffett Industrial Park, was owned by developers Richard Peery and John Arrillaga and comprised eighty buildings with another twenty planned. A decade later, Peery and Arrillaga sold 48 of their buildings in Sunnyvale to Aetna Life and Casualty Company and Koll Construction Company for $50 million. Western Electric Corporation, located north of Arques between Lawrence Expressway and Wolfe, bought an additional twenty-three acres at the International Science Center. At about the same time, Southern Pacific formed a joint venture partnership with the City of Sunnyvale and the City of Santa Clara to develop Oakmead Industrial Park on 370 acres at Lawrence and Central expressways that had been the source of contention over a General Motors facility in the 1950s.

As it did with so many other streets, the city wanted to widen North Mary Avenue. Industrial real estate developers had plans for property adjacent to a five-and-a-half acre chrysanthemum farm owned by the Takagi family. The son, Fred Takagi, was torn between the economic security that selling the land would provide and the family tradition of farming.

> Ninety-nine percent of the growers aren't in this for business reasons . . . . They really just want to grow flowers. But the younger guys, like myself, are more inclined to look at it from the business standpoint.[5]

Slowly but surely, the last bits of open space were sold and developed.

Another Sunnyvale chrysanthemum farmer on North Mary Avenue, Mr. Y. K. Fong, was a Chinese immigrant from Macao, a Portuguese colony off the coast of mainland China, who came to Sunnyvale in 1960. Fong's son and daughter claimed that "quick talking developers have abused Asian-American farmers," and that their father's limited English caused him to agree with developers' proposals. When Mary Manor Mobile Home Park was built next to the Fong farm, Mr. Fong attempted to object because he worried that if people moved in, they would be bothered by the insecticides he sprayed on his flowers. His objections were ignored by developers, but the new residents were quick to complain during spraying season. Fong's son Paul made a bid for city council in 1975 as a way to make the voices of Asian-Americans and farmers heard.[6] Opponent Harold Shields claimed Paul Fong should be disqualified from running for city council because he had only lived within city limits for one year prior to the election. Before that, Fong had lived at his father's North Mary Avenue property which was as yet unincorporated. Fong eventually threw his support to Larry Stone and dropped out of the race.

George Nakano, another flower grower, had owned 17 acres near the intersection of Reed Avenue and Wolfe Road since 1950 when he planted his own chrysanthemum farm on three of the acres. He leased the rest to James and Shigeyo Imahara, who planted strawberries and tomatoes. When Nakano bought the land in 1950, his property tax bill was $73, and by 1976 he was paying $14,000 annually. Paperwork required by local, state and federal governments for farmers became more demanding and complicated with each passing year. When Nakano decided to sell the property to real estate developer Victor Bellomo in 1976, an agricultural land preservation bill was before the state senate. Nakano and Bellomo both vehemently opposed any regulation, maintaining that property owners needed to be able to be compensated for their investment in land.

Bellomo himself had been a cherry orchardist until he sold his land in the 1960s and went into the property development business. Nakano sold the strawberry patch to Bellomo who had a waiting list with 250 names for sixty-seven houses in "Strawberry Gardens" which sold for between $73,000 and $87,000. The Imaharas, who had leased fourteen acres since 1955, were forced to let their twenty field hands go. Imahara regretted the sale: "They say this is progress, but I don't know. In ten more days these tomatoes would have been ready for the harvest."[7] The Imaharas eventually opened a produce store.

City officials were not about to curb development though. In 1972, a citizens' group proposed rezoning 200 acres of land adjacent to the Orchard Gardens neighborhood which had been earmarked for industry. Orchard Gardens was a residential island and was isolated from other neighborhoods by industrial development. Residents advocated the change because a new school would be required and their children would not have to continue to commute to school. The unanimous council vote against the proposal outraged citizens because it appeared that the council had decided their position before any public debate. A new school was out of the question and by the late 1970s, Sunnyvale School District had closed one intermediate and five elementary schools.

The city did, however, attempt to provide more community services. A community relations department was established and Sunnyvale Community Center, a multi-purpose recreation facility on twenty acres, was completed in 1973. Part of the land was formerly the Pavlina family's orchard. The giant old oak tree, which remains there today, shaded generations of orchard workers and once held an old rope swing where the Pavlina children played.[8]

For twenty years, Sunnyvale had proclaimed the benefits of a strong industrial presence in Sunnyvale. That presence consisted primarily of defense-oriented businesses until the end of the Vietnam War when defense contracts dropped off. City officials scrambled to find developers who were building for consumer-oriented high-tech companies.

They bemoaned the short-sighted reliance on the defense department and launched an entirely new welcome campaign to high-technology businesses. City Manager John Dever recalled "then the stress was on defense-oriented industry where drastic cutbacks occurred. I don't think we'll be quite as vulnerable as we were."[9] He felt that consumer high-technology businesses would offer more economic stability than defense contractors.

A liberal citizens lobby group, ORCHARDS (Organization of Responsible Citizens to Halt Reckless Development in Sunnyvale), opposed further industrial development, defense-oriented or otherwise and sought to open city government to greater citizen involvement. Ironically, despite the acronym, ninety percent of the orchards were already replaced by residential and industrial development. ORCHARDS sponsored three candidates for city council in 1973: Gisela Daetz, Beth Erickson and Charles Duke. The candidates believed that unrestrained development was not best serving the public interest. Councilman Charles Hefferlin claimed that "what is happening [development] is a source of pride and gratification, no matter what the reason, because the end result is providing relocating [sic] of jobs through diversification."[10] Councilman Charley Allen called the ORCHARDS candidates "neophytes" who created issues rather than dealing with real problems.

Incumbent Mayor Etta S. Albert warned the public against the "radical element," referring to ORCHARDS members, when she spoke at the Sunnyvale Republican Women's Club lunch shortly before the election: "If you want another Berkeley or another Palo Alto, the future of Sunnyvale is in your hands, with the people you elect."[11] Although none of the ORCHARDS candidates was successful in 1973, they made a respectable showing.

The development debate continued after ORCHARDS' electoral defeat. ORCHARDS chairman Larry Stone said that "development is just out of control. It's rampant." Mayor Albert's response was:

I don't see what he's talking about in saying develop-

ment is rampant. Sunnyvale is regarded widely as one of the better planned cities in this area. And we are 98% developed already. Development here has been controlled, not rampant.[12]

In 1975 elections, two ORCHARDS candidates won seats on the city council. Larry Stone, a Santa Clara County planning commissioner, defeated incumbent and former Mayor Harold Shields. Greg Morris, an attorney and founding member of ORCHARDS, won the seat vacated by former Mayor Charles Hefferlin. ORCHARDS, and Larry Stone in particular, became an anathema to longtime council member and former Mayor Don Koreski who tried to block no-growth proposals and other policies proposed by ORCHARDS. Koreski retired because term limits were imposed in 1977 and because of his increasing frustration with ORCHARDS council members.

Regional relationships and Sunnyvale's relationship to county government became more important. County Supervisor Dan McCorquodale of the third district came out in support of ORCHARDS candidates because he felt Sunnyvale had a history of stormy relations with county government. He hoped Sunnyvale would adopt less isolationist policies. Charley Allen suggested a "convention" of city councils within the county and county government officials. However, City Manager Dever felt the county's power was encroaching on local decisions and he refused to participate in some county-wide activities, including the 1975 county census. During Dever's tenure county-municipal relations were not always cordial.

ORCHARDS advocated purchasing land for open space. A November 1974 ballot measure authorized the sale of $5 million worth of 20-year general obligation bonds for purchase of open space. Etta Albert did not want the measure on the ballot because

the general public [does not have] the information available, the background, the knowledge of bond markets, and so on, available to the council and staff to be able to make these kinds of decisions.[13]

ORCHARDS' new wave of politicians wanted to open this kind of decision to the public.

Downtown redevelopment continued to be a major issue for the city council particularly since the seven city council members also made up the Sunnyvale Redevelopment Agency. Town & Country Village had not been the panacea for blight and age in downtown that everyone expected. Hart's Department Store closed its 63,000 square foot store at Sunnyvale Plaza in early 1975. Nevertheless, Don Logan, who ran unopposed for his council seat in 1975 and held two consecutive terms as mayor, advocated additional redevelopment like the Town & Country Village. He claimed that "if we don't do it now, we'll just have a crappy downtown forever."[14]

The identity crisis facing Sunnyvale in the 1960s carried through the following decade. San José State University professor Michael Otten analyzed the community to study the relationship between Public Safety officers and the public. Besides finding a positive police/public relationship, Otten concluded that Sunnyvale was "a loose community where people do not seem to have a strong sense of belonging. . ."[15] He cited rapid growth, Sunnyvale's location near San José and just south of Stanford University, and the transient nature of many of the jobs in the area as the major factors contributing to over 30% of the respondents not being able to identify the name of their neighborhood.

The growing obsolescence of the central area prompted the planning department to contract an economic feasibility study of the downtown retail area. It was recommended that a new regional shopping center be built. The 1975 total assessed value of downtown was $2,058,560; market value, however, was $12,557,216.[16] An environmental impact report describing the area proposed four alternatives as approaches to downtown redevelopment. The first was partial redevelopment, which included enclosing the existing Sunnyvale Plaza in a mall and adding two additional anchor tenants. The second alternative was to continue patchwork rehabilitation to salvage downtown, but pursue no massive redevelopment. Third, the report proposed combining commercial and residental development to create an urban center rather than a shopping center. The fourth alternative was to improve parking and landscaping, but no further renewal. Remarkably, neither the environmental impact report nor the economic feasibility study mentioned four existing Sunnyvale neighborhood shopping centers: Cherry Chase Center, Pavlina Plaza, Loehman's Plaza and La Hacienda Shopping Center, whose combined retail space totaled 400,000 square feet. In addition, more than 100,000 square feet of retail space was already under construction at the Homestead Square Shopping Center. An earlier study prepared by Victor Gruen Associates recommended extensive use of pedestrian walkways to grid the area from the civic center to the retail center. None of the alternatives proposed were implemented, instead a much more radical approach was taken.

In June 1976, the Sunnyvale City Council sat as the Sunnyvale Redevelopment Agency and adopted a preliminary development agreement and financing package to develop a regional shopping mall in Sunnyvale's downtown. Councilman Don Koreski abstained because of a conflict of interest since he owned property downtown, and Councilman Larry Stone cast the only dissenting vote claiming the project was too big. He wanted to convince Ernest Hahn, the general partner and developer, that Sunnyvale did not need such a massive regional shopping center. Councilwoman Etta Albert-Logan, who had recently married Mayor Don Logan, claimed the center was "exactly what is needed," and Councilman Gil Gunn said he could no longer tolerate the empty stores, sex shops, and traffic problems downtown. According to Gunn, the center was inevitable and "We can't do anything to stop this development!"[17]

A representative of the citizens' group ORCHARDS complained to a packed council meeting that the proposed report was so confusing that it may as well have been written in "Mandarin Chinese." He questioned reliability of the financial proposals for the project, and asked whether

ABOVE: *Demolition of Stevens fabric store in old downtown, 1978. Courtesy Edwina Brackenbury.* RIGHT: *Anthony Popovich's furniture store, Armanini's Drug and Store, J.J. Newberry's, downtown Sunnyvale just before demolition to make way for the shopping mall. Courtesy Ann Zarko.*

city funds would be needed to pay obligations on the bonds. Larry Stone raised concerns about the use of general city funds, but he eventually supported the financial package even though he objected to the size of the project. City Manager Dever assured all that there would be no financial risk for the city.[18] In October 1976, Sunnyvale officials agreed to undertake the Sunnyvale Town Center project by contracting with a partnership of builder Ernest W. Hahn,

Inc., and Sunnyvale Town Center Properties Corporation, a R. H. Macy & Co. subsidiary.

Some felt betrayed by Larry Stone, who in their view, did not continue to fight the redevelopment project. Stone believed that his early dissenting vote made his position clear, but refusing to participate in decision-making on the project would not be in the best interest of the city.[19] Residents for a Vote on Redevelopment formed to continue to oppose the project and their platform asserted that anticipated revenues from the center were overstated and liabilities underestimated. They launched an unsuccessful campaign for a referendum. Councilwoman Albert-Logan called the residents "poor losers" and went on to say, "I guess the only way you can convert people like that is to get them elected to the city council." Her reference pointed to Larry Stone, in her view, a converted ORCHARDS council member.[20]

Sunnyvale Plaza, slightly more than twenty years old, was demolished in 1977, including almost thirty-five acres covering nine city blocks with ninety individual land parcels of residential units, eighty-four retail outlets, forty-nine commercial businesses, ten financial organizations and five non-profit groups. What had been the core of Sunnyvale was leveled and by all appearances, a bomb had been dropped, creating a huge gash in the heart of the city. Sunnyvale's persona was forever altered and the former farm community was a distant memory for the few who could remember. The visual landscape held no clues to Sunnyvale's history.

The "Heart Transplant for Sunnyvale," was described in a June 1978 article in Peninsula Magazine. "Residents and visitors to Sunnyvale are trying to adjust to the annihilation of the downtown they had known where streets have disappeared and businesses were displaced."[21] Unfortunately, the heart of the town did not seem to be transplanted, but simply eradicated. There is no one place in Sunnyvale that residents uniformly point to as the heart of the city.

A few trees survived the obliteration of downtown and they owe their survival to a little old lady who stood before "bulldozers of progress," refusing to let the trees be destroyed. Fern Ohrt, who as a child had been inspired when she heard John Muir speak, researched the origin of each of the trees on the property of what once had been Sunnyvale's City Hall.[22] She discovered that when the old city hall was completed in the early 1930s, there was no available money for landscaping. Local school children

Trees that were saved largely by the efforts of Fern Ohrt are visible as construction gets underway on Sunnyvale Town Center. Courtesy Edwina Brackenbury.

collected coins and purchased one of the cedar trees planted there under the direction of Mayor Fred Drew. The Sunnyvale Women's Club planted a second cedar, and buried a time capsule at its base. In the 1920s, a Sunnyvale man, Mr. Svitz, had smuggled two redwood saplings into California from Oregon and planted them near his Washington Street home. When he heard that the city hall needed trees, he transplanted them to the city property because he knew they would grow too big for his yard. Two other redwood trees had marked either side of a driveway when they were planted. Today they appear very close together. Fern Ohrt was a witness when the last tree was planted on city hall land on Memorial Day in 1945 by some Sunnyvale war mothers. The day the tree was planted, an auto accident in front of Fremont High School claimed the lives of two other Sunnyvale boys, making the tree an even more poignant memorial.

Fern Ohrt believed Sunnyvale made a huge mistake when they agreed to tear apart the entire downtown. She said the city "had a City Manager [Dever] who only knew

Fern Ohrt, the "tree lady" who pestered city council to save the old cedar and redwood trees and incorporate them into the design of Sunnyvale Town Center. Courtesy Sunnyvale Historical Society & Museum Association

John Dever

how to tear down, chop down and bulldoze, and they thought he was God."[23] When she went before the city council to plead a reprieve for the trees, the 81-year-old told the council she preferred to have their promise to use the trees in the design of the mall "in writing." The spunky woman became known around city call as the "tree lady." The shopping mall ultimately was designed and constructed around the trees and the middle of the mall is an open plaza. For her work in preserving the old trees, Mrs. Ohrt was awarded both "Citizen of the Year" by the city and the "Good Apple" from the Sunnyvale School District.

City Manager John Dever had many supporters, however, and was congratulated on his development policies when he won two prestigious awards from the International City Management Association (ICMA), the first time one person was awarded both accolades from that organization in one year. The following year, Dever accepted an job offer from the city of Long Beach to be their city manager. Lee Ayres was hired to replace John Dever.

Sunnyvale Town Center, a $60 million regional mall, opened in September 1979. The shopping center was intended to draw shoppers from well beyond the boundaries

of Sunnyvale. The Town Center project was financed by the Sunnyvale Redevelopment Agency which sold bonds to private investors. In 1977, bonds valued at $38,000,000 were issued. Proceeds were used for property acquisition, relocation expenses, demolition costs, and public improvements, including a two-story parking structure.

California's infamous Proposition 13 had profound impact in Sunnyvale because it changed many variables in the shopping mall equation. It cut property taxes on which the city counted to retire the bonds which had been sold to support the mall and, at the same time, benefited developers of Town Center by reducing interest rates by two-thirds. Sunnyvale incurred an annual loss of $1.6 million on bond

Sunnyvale Town Center

payments and the city made unsuccessful attempts to recoup their losses from the developers' windfall. City officials claimed that the debts would be reduced when a third major tenant leased space. Additional shortfalls were due to the fact that a third anchor tenant for the mall did not materialize until 1992 when J. C. Penney opened.

Redevelopment Agency Director Gordon Miller asserted in 1978 that the impetus for downtown redevelopment had come from the Downtown Business and Professional Association. Councilman Larry Stone claimed that the project had been the brainchild of then City Manager John Dever. When residents looked at what had formerly been the downtown and asked "What happened?" or "Who did this?" there was no easy answer and certainly no consensus of opinion. Certainly the lack of public participation at the early stages of the decision-making process was a contributing factor. By the time the project began, however, many downtown merchants who initially were supportive, opposed the mall. They accused developer Ernest Hahn of underhanded tactics to eliminate any competition for his handpicked tenants. Others realized that their rent would be increased as much as 500%, and changed their opinion of the shopping mall.

One such merchant, Michael Lenhart, an immigrant from Yugoslavia in 1960, had a downtown Sunnyvale business selling wigs. When he was notified of the impending demise of his building, he plastered huge signs on all the windows proclaiming "Forced out of business by City of Sunnyvale and Macy's," and "My Three Children May Go Hungry" and "How Free is America?"[24] Paul and Lisa Staschower, owners of Paul's Draperies, filed a lawsuit in an attempt to hold up the project, but a superior court judge refused to hear the case.[25] Eve Marshall, a local resident, cut her Macy's charge card in several pieces and sent them to the store's headquarters. The president of Macy's called her and asked if he could reissue her card. She refused and said she would not shop at the mall. She urged the other 125 people at a May 1978 city council meeting to cut up their charge cards too.[26]

As the shopping mall was built, rumors abounded that city officials had even more plans to turn the 1,000-acre central core, which contained over two thousand single-family homes, into a redevelopment project for high-density housing and offices. A public hearing was held at Adair School the night of March 22, 1978 and was attended by business people and 200 angry residents who suspected the city planned to raze their old homes. Former Chamber of Commerce Manager Al Spiers was present and was applauded by the crowd when he emotionally demanded to know why "brand new businesses" at Sunnyvale Plaza were torn down to make way for the shopping mall when "skid row" on Murphy Avenue was left untouched. He was so agitated while speaking that he collapsed and was pronounced dead when he was taken by ambulance to El Camino Hospital. The following week, city officials at-

Construction of Sunnyvale Town Center shopping mall, 1978. Courtesy Edwina Brackenbury.

tempted to soothe public sentiment when they sent out a letter with assurances that there was no "master plan" for the area, and invited comments or proposals from the citizens.

One vocal opponent of the shopping mall and any threats to the old neighborhoods was Alillion Wilhelmy, a school teacher whose late husband had been mayor in the early 1930s. She decried the destruction of old city hall because the building, in her eyes, had been usable and very attractive. She thought it wasteful that homes were lost to build Sunnyvale Town Center. The thought that her own neighborhood around Frances Avenue would be rezoned for high density residential development lit a fire under her and she joined the committee to "Save Our Homes." Mrs. Wilhelmy, or "Willie" as she was known to friends and neighbors, walked door-to-door to speak to everyone she could to avert rezoning. Although by this time she was already an elderly woman, she did not sit quietly at city council meetings, but spoke passionately and articulately about the value of the old neighborhood. Her success can be measured by the 1980 zoning restrictions against high density housing in her neighborhood which today is a Heritage Housing District.

Many other Sunnyvaleans agreed with Willie, and an increasing number took interest in the historic heritage of the city. Manuel Vargas or "Mr. Sunnyvale," as he was named because of his hundreds of historical presentations to local school children, had been involved in the effort to save the old Murphy family house and was an active member and past president of the Sunnyvale Historical Society and Museum Association. Manuel and his wife Mary lived their whole lives in Sunnyvale, and having been married in 1914, were honored in 1979 at the Santa Clara County Fair as the longest married couple in the county.

Likewise one-time Sunnyvale Historical Society President Pat Malone rallied local history buffs into action with his idea to rebuild a replica of the old Murphy house as a historical museum for the city. He went so far as to have San José architect Ken Rodriques draw plans, and launched fund-raisers to bring his dream to reality. The idea never materialized, but his enthusiasm for Sunnyvale's early history inspired many others.

Some of Sunnyvale's landmarks did gain attention, however. In 1978, the American Society of Mechanical Engineers declared Joshua Hendy Iron Works a National Historic Engineering Landmark, honoring the technical evolution that occurred due to the many accomplishments at Hendy and Westinghouse. Today it is the site of the Iron Man Museum which features exhibits depicting products of the two companies and highlighting the history of mechanical technology.

Although most neighborhoods had been absorbed within the city limits by the 1970s, several small "islands" were still under the jurisdiction of the county. In 1978, the city attempted to annex over 400 acres with 2,500 residents. Since the pockets of land were smaller than 100 acres each, it was not necessary for a vote by the residents. Raynor Park neighbors unsuccessfully fought annexation by the City of Sunnyvale, and to this day, many residents resent the annexation action taken by the city.

By the end of the decade, 65,000 non-residents worked in the city's seven industrial parks. The commuting work force had very little personal, social, cultural or political connection to the City of Sunnyvale. The presence of the Silicon Valley was clear by the number of buildings sprouting up at an incredible rate to house high-tech companies but what had been the "heart" of the town no longer existed. Instead there was a shopping mall, which in the mind of cherry farmer Ruel Olson was "a monument to the concrete industry."[27] There remained severe fragmentation in the city's constituencies of former farmers, merchants, longtime residents, new entrepreneurs and elected officials. The apparent divisiveness was a symptom of the community attempting to redefine its identity.

Chapter 8

THE HEART
OF SILICON VALLEY

The Silicon Valley phenomenon was a major social, economic and cultural influence on the entire Santa Clara Valley. Sunnyvale became identified as the "heart" of the computer industry sprawl because it was home to more high-tech companies than any other city in the world. By 1980, the press acknowledged Sunnyvale's position as the "heart":

> Thanks to its unbridled industrial growth, Sunnyvale has earned the nickname "The Heart of the Silicon Valley." A greater concentration of high-technology businesses has developed there than anywhere else in the world.[1]

It is ironic that a city that had just undergone a "heart transplant" was perceived as the heart of the electronics industry.

During the late 1970s and early 1980s, Silicon Valley and therefore Sunnyvale, became a magnet to people from all parts of the world, particularly Asia and the Pacific Rim, as a place to work and live. Thousands streamed into Santa Clara County with this modern-day gold fever to find their own personal success in the electronics revolution. The 1980 census indicated 63% more Asians in the county than in 1975.[2] San Jose Mercury News editor Bob Ingle called the influx of immigrants "a demographic revolution" and by offering an eight-part series entitled "Faces of the Future," called for an examination of "our multi-cultural community."[3]

Andrew Grove, president of Intel Corporation, and himself an immigrant from Hungary, gives insight into the choices of the newcomers.

> For a lot of these immigrants — myself being an example of this — technology is a way to break into the mainstream, middle-class American society, because technology and technological work are less dependent on language skills.[4]

Some highly educated recent immigrants filled the highest positions in companies, but the majority filled the lowest paying jobs. The new high-tech industry demanded both skilled and unskilled workers, a phenomenon which set it apart from older, traditional industries which rarely had demand for large numbers of highly educated professionals. The emerging industry needed "intellectually qualified manpower while at the same time . . . access to substantial pools of unskilled labor."[5]

School district statistics reflected the demographic changes when more than 50% of Sunnyvale students identified themselves as "minority" whose primary language was not English. The percentage of minority residents in Sunnyvale is smaller than both Santa Clara County and California as a whole. However, a higher percentage of Asians lives in Sunnyvale than in either the state or the county.[6]

The demeanor of the city council was markedly different from earlier years as the influence of ORCHARDS became apparent. By 1980 urban planner Dianne McKenna was mayor, and the other council members were primarily young, career-oriented people whose political perspectives included a vision beyond the city limits. John Mercer, for example, was involved with the National League of Cities and Dianne McKenna was a member of various Bay Area and county commissions. The isolationism of the previous decade, fostered by former City Manager John Dever, began to give way to greater efforts at regional communication. Two of Sunnyvale's mayors from that era, Ron Gonzales and Dianne McKenna, went on to serve as county supervisors, taking the benefit of their municipal experience to the county level.

At the beginning of the 1980s, a change in the traditional pro-growth attitude became obvious in Sunnyvale. The city had grown so quickly that council members and citizens alike began to take a long look at their city and evaluate what had taken place in the previous thirty years. In January 1980, for the first time in the history of Sunnyvale and possibly the first in the state, the city council invoked a

Dianne McKenna

Larry Stone and Ron Gonzales

112-day moratorium on industrial growth. Councilwoman Lynn Briody proposed the "pause" to examine the impact of growth on transportation and housing, and to look for ways

Lynn Briody

to solve some of the problems facing the city.[7] The suspension in industrial building was intended to allow time for recommendations to be drawn up to have industries pay part of the cost of mitigating traffic congestion and housing shortages. Variances to the moratorium were granted for 500,000 square feet of building space already underway, but the council made the point that *carte blanche* development was a thing of the past. The chamber of commerce, however, openly criticized and opposed the moratorium, claiming that a no-growth policy was not in Sunnyvale's best interest.[8]

The "time out" mood of the council was reflective of many residents. The shock of the metamorphosis of downtown had set in and people began to reexamine the choices that had been made. The focal point of this reflection became the only block still standing of old downtown: the 100 block of Murphy Avenue. While the street had been the pulse of the community in the 1940s and 1950s and before, it lost its vitality when shoppers went to Taaffe Street's Sunnyvale Plaza a few blocks away in the 1960s. Subsequently Murphy Avenue became the scene of a string of barrooms and pornographic book and film shops, definitely not the pride of the community. Ironically, the 100 block of Murphy Avenue had survived only by accident. It had been slated to be razed, but Federal urban renewal dollars could not be used for commercial streets and disallowed it from the Encina Urban Renewal Project. Despite politicians' attempts to eliminate what they perceived to be blight, consultants

"Apple Annie's" took over the old bank building. Courtesy Ann Zarko.

recommended against demolition, fearing the land would lie vacant for years to come. Estimates to demolish the street came in at $16 million while bids to renovate were about $3 million. The tired, old street found new friends in the 1980s, through a campaign spearheaded by local resident Ann Hines who pointed out original architectural features in the buildings which were simply hidden by "improvements" over the years. Hines rallied Murphy Avenue merchants to lobby the city in an effort to save the street and they formed the Murphy Station Business Association (MSBA).[9]

In the wake of downtown redevelopment, a new appreciation emerged that "progress" did not necessarily mean wholesale destruction of old structures. The city established a citizen committee called the Heritage Preservation Commission to advise the city council on historic resources. Alillion Wilhelmy, who had spent endless hours campaigning to save her own neighborhood, was named to the first commission, as was Ann Hines who had formerly served on Santa Clara County's Heritage Commission and was largely responsible for the city's adoption of a comprehensive preservation plan. One of the first tasks delegated to the new commission was to create a Cultural Resource Inventory which identified those structures and trees of historic value to the city so that efforts could be made to preserve them. The Santa Clara County Heritage Preservation Commission honored Sunnyvale with an award for "Excellence in Historic Preservation" commending its preservation efforts.

In 1981 Murphy Avenue was declared a Heritage Landmark District, which gave the city greater control over renovations or reconstructions of the vintage 1920s buildings. This is perhaps the first instance in the city's history when the least invasive measure was chosen. The transformation of the street to a conglomeration of restaurants, book stores, galleries alongside Kirkish's Western Wear and traditional shoe repair and barber shops was an attempt to plan for the future by capitalizing on the past.

This shift toward a more historic-minded community coincided with the 1981 centennial observance of the "grandest party the West had ever seen," the 50th anniversary bash of Mary and Martin Murphy, Jr. The Sunnyvale Historical Society joined forces with the city to sponsor a three-day centennial barbecue celebration, on the weekend of July 17, 1981, recreating the Murphy clan's festivities of one hundred years earlier. The event was the brainchild of then historical society President Pat Malone, always eager to regale listeners with stories of the past, and was executed by hundreds of volunteers under the management of Ann Hines, who headed up the centennial barbecue committee. Manuel Vargas acted as the Honorary Grand Marshall of the event.[10]

The weekend opened with a Friday night Heritage Ball at the community center and many party goers donned period costume. Saturday's parade drew spectators, many of whom arrived on the specially arranged trains from San

Pat Malone, one-time President of Sunnyvale Historical Society & Museum Association at the centennial celebration of the "grandest party the West has ever seen," July 17-19, 1981. Courtesy Sunnyvale Historical Society & Museum Associaton.

tours, college workshops, teacher in-services, and particularly "Hands on History" where close to 1,000 Sunnyvale elementary school children visit the historical museum each year to get firsthand experience with such items as a clothes ringer, a cherry pitter, a butter churn and various other artifacts on special display. Peterson often refers to her friend Sandy Lydon's theory of "the dancing web of history," where our individual pasts are often interwoven together with larger events and in studying the past we are made aware of what links us together.[11] Over the years, numerous

Kay Peterson, photo by Erica Austin.

José and San Francisco just as they had one hundred years earlier. Upon disembarking from the train, they were serenaded by a brass band. A traditional California barbecue was held both Saturday and Sunday featuring tri-tip steaks, roasted over oak. Horse and buggy rides and Wells Fargo stage coach added to the old-fashioned atmosphere. Twelve Sunnyvale couples celebrating their 50th wedding anniversaries were special guests of honor for the entire weekend. Although historic consciousness-raising is difficult to measure, without a doubt, many Sunnyvale citizens went home with a new appreciation of what and whom had gone before, and a fresh outlook on the city they call home.

Local history was not completely new to everyone, and one particular retired Sunnyvale school teacher has made it her vocation to instill an appreciation of early town life in both children and adult students. Kay Peterson, initially an environmental conservationist, has spent the last two decades bringing history to life by leading walking

volunteers from the historical society have served as docents and tour guides for the children's "Hands on History."

The Sunnyvale Historical Society and Museum Association continues to offer presentations, docent-led tours to school children and adults, a walking tour of Murphy Avenue and lends support to private citizens making efforts to rescue historic buildings from the wrecking ball. The society rallies support from a broad-base of residents who favor larger quarters for the historical museum. The museum collection has been carefully tended and has grown over the years. It consists of hundreds of historic photographs, thousands of artifacts ranging from Murphy family furniture and portraits to Moffett Field memorabilia. The museum also boasts a valuable archive of pamphlets, newspapers, property deeds and public works blueprints.

Even real estate developers played a part in preserving architectural bits of the past. In 1982, Lincoln Property Company bought the former Libby, McNeil, & Libby cannery site and by 1985 had turned it into the 500,000 square foot Sunnyvale Industrial Park. The developers were required to save the towering fruit cocktail can, in earlier days a disguise for a water tower. They commissioned artist Anita Kaplan to restore the "can" to its 1935 fruit cocktail label and integrated it into the industrial park landscape.[12] The landmark remains today a reminder of Libby's and the cannery work that once was carried out at that site.

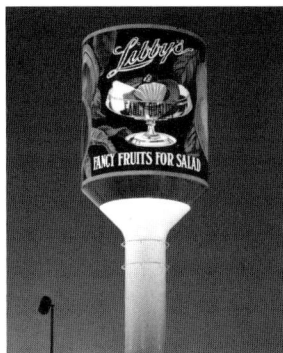

Former Libby Cannery water tower disguised as a fruit cocktail can, refurbished by Anita Kaplan. Courtesy City of Sunnyvale.

Every building or tree of historic value has not been saved, however. In 1985, the William Wurster-designed office and administration building for Schuckl's cannery was demolished to make way for high-density residential units at Fair Oaks and Evelyn avenues. Architectural experts had acclaimed the building as "likely to be remembered as one of the incomparable business buildings of the twentieth century,"[13] but to no avail. The structure was all but hidden by the Fair Oaks overpass built in the 1960s. "Brutally buried under the new overpass, its urban setting in a once small town at the exposed corner of the great fruit canning works can only be imagined today."[14] There are condos in its place, and it really cannot be imagined today.

The military-industrial complex which had such a strong presence in Sunnyvale since World War II, faced significant cutbacks as fewer tax dollars were allocated for defense projects. The Navy withdrew from Moffett Field in the first few years of the 1990s, and debate ensued over future use of the base. Local citizenry were almost unanimous in their opposition to turning the base into a general aviation airport. Councilwoman Robin Parker voiced their concerns when she chaired the Sunnyvale-Mountain View Joint Committee on the future of Moffett Field. The Air Force chose to retain use of their "Blue Cube" and will gradually take over family housing units formerly used by the Navy. Many local residents had no idea the Air Force had a presence near Moffett, but with the thaw of the Cold War, the top-secret status of their projects has been reduced. The Sunnyvale Air Force Station was renamed Onizuka Air Force Base in honor of Lt. Col. Ellison Onizuka, one of seven killed in the 1986 *Challenger* space shuttle disaster.

Shrinking defense expenditures translated very clearly into loss of jobs for thousands in Santa Clara County. In the early 1990s, many defense industry workers turned to the North Valley Private Industry Council (NOVA) for retraining in order to find work in new or emerging industries. NOVA was formed in 1983 as part of the Federal Job Training Partnership Act. Initially it focused its efforts on job training for youth, seniors, and the handicapped. NOVA, which is managed by the City of Sunnyvale, tailored itself to handle thousands of laid-off workers and victims of corporate "downsizing." The award-winning program drew national attention in 1993 when President Bill Clinton and Vice President Al Gore visited NOVA's STAR (Skills Testing, Assessment and Referral) center which helped over 5,000 that year to write resumes, interview, retrain, and find new work. NOVA maintains a waiting list almost as long as the number served each year.

Sunnyvale's city managers and city councils through the 1970s and 1980s attempted to guide the city through the fast-paced demographic changes in the valley. Careful attention needed to be paid to fiscal issues so that city services could be maintained for the growing population. Since the mid-1970s, Sunnyvale has used performance-based budgeting in public safety, and subsequently in other departments. Tom Lewcock, who took over the city Manager's job from Lee Ayers in the late-1970s, reinforced pay for performance, basing managers' pay on the performance of their respective departments. Likewise, when the city council is budgeting, it makes decisions on service levels. It decides whether it is worth cutting or enhancing present service levels, not whether to hire or fire one or more people. The system also calls for calculating the cost of operational or capital enhancements over a ten year period,

Thomas Lewcock

allowing for more accurate long-range financial planning. The "system" focuses on results and rewards efficiency, running the municipal government like a business.

Both Lewcock and one-time Mayor and Councilman John Mercer became spokespeople for Sunnyvale's budget style, that even in the wake of California's Prop 13 had the city with 35% fewer employees than other cities of its size. Speaking before a city administrators meeting in San Antonio, Texas in 1986, they explained their view of Sunnyvale as a "municipal corporation," which seeks to reward efficiency and penalize waste.[15] Facilitating performance-based budgeting is a city computer system which tracks employee tasks allowing the city to determine how many hours to devote to given jobs. It is not surprising that a city taking pride in being "the heart of Silicon Valley" was a pioneer in municipal governments to go "on-line." In 1991 both Mercer and Lewcock were invited to explain Sunnyvale's budget model to the Senate Governmental Affairs Committee in Washington, D. C., giving Sunnyvale national recognition. Mercer went to work in the nation's capital, first for the Department of Housing and Urban Development (HUD), and then for a committee which helped author the Government Performance and Results Act legislation (signed by

President Clinton in 1993), which sets performance goals for several federal agencies. Mercer wanted to turn "Sunnyvale into a national role model."[16]

Subsequently, Sunnyvale was cited as an example of successful municipal budgeting in David Osborne and Ted Gaebler's Reinventing Government,[17] a book popular with the Clinton Administration. Sunnyvale was also highlighted on ABC's "World News Tonight" national broadcast late in 1992, featuring the pay-for-performance model. Both the national news coverage and the citation in Reinventing Government caught the attention of the Clinton Administration and Sunnyvale enjoyed the national spotlight when the president visited Sunnyvale in 1993.

Some critics of Sunnyvale's performance-based budgeting and the notoriety it has received claim that "democratic vitality" is lost because the department managers exercise so much control.[18] The criticism is an ironic twist since the budgeting system came into play in Sunnyvale just as ORCHARDS candidates were elected in the 1970s. A plank of their platform had been to open local government to broader public participation, certainly not intending to diminish "democratic vitality."

Other cities often face conflict between city management and law enforcement, but Sunnyvale's public safety director until 1992, Jess Barba, worked closely with City Manager Tom Lewcock in developing cooperative, comprehensive city services. The two co-authored an article entitled "Managers and Police Chiefs: Friends or Foes?" which outlined their cooperative philosophies. Lewcock noted the need for a city manager to clearly identify his or her expectations from a police chief, all the while giving support for field tactical operations decisions. Barba emphasized personal trust between professionals, without which "the overall mission, or good of the city or county, becomes subordinate to game playing, distrust, and strategizing to prevail for the sake of ego defense or protection of turf."[19]

The 1980s in Sunnyvale were not as turbulent politically or socially as previous decades had been. Council members, while sometimes disagreeing, for the most part did not engage in personal political battles as in the previous two decades. Until the "garbage war," their relationship with constituents was generally smooth.

Early in 1990, Sunnyvale City Council voted to award a ten year contract to the non-union Los Gatos-based Green Valley Disposal Company to collect garbage in the city. Green Valley's bid was millions of dollars lower over the ten year period, than the next lowest bidder. Specialty Garbage, a family-owned and union represented Sunnyvale company founded by August Lewis in the 1920s as Sunnyvale Garbage Company and later run by his son Harry, had collected Sunnyvale's trash for sixty years, with nary a complaint. However, the multi-million dollar savings was tempting to the budget-conscious city council and they voted to contract with Green Valley.

The political fall-out from their vote caught the council by surprise, as residents whose ire was raised, came from all over the city to protest the council's acceptance of the lower bid. Supporters of Specialty collected 14,000 signatures to initiate a referendum election which left the council and neighboring cities wondering how a lower bid could generate such highly charged emotions from the electorate. Support for the home town company, particularly by older voters, was vastly underestimated by the council and ultimately, the contract was re-awarded to Specialty. Evidently most residents did not believe that Green Valley could do an adequate job with such a low bid. On a more emotional level, Sunnyvale residents wanted to support a longtime local company that was union and family-run. Ironically, Specialty Garbage Company became available for sale in 1992 and Green Valley expressed interest, although did not buy it.

If the war waged over garbage collection was not enough to send political shock waves through Sunnyvale, the accusation of sexual molestation leveled against Mayor Brian O'Toole was. The end of 1990 was a sad chapter in city politics when the up-and-coming politically successful thirty-five-year-old Brian O'Toole pleaded no contest and was sentenced to six years in prison. Councilman Richard Napier took O'Toole's position as mayor.

In many respects, the late-1970s and 1980s were the Larry Stone era in Sunnyvale politics. The outspoken and controversial councilman and two-time mayor gained many friends and foes in his eighteen years in municipal politics. While he may be best known for his part in ORCHARDS, his greatest legacy may prove to be his unwavering support of the arts. Although his ardent appeals to build a $25 million performing arts center did not sway enough constituents or

Larry Stone

fellow council members, his stance on the arts has benefited the community. Public purchase and display of works of art was developed and enhanced during the Stone era. As he explained in a 1988 speech:

> *As elected officials we must recognize that art is from the middle. It is fundamental, basic to our lives and, indeed, to a civilized society . . . . Look at the support that local government gives to baseball from Little Leagues to adult softball. If we did that for the arts in this nation, what a land of musicians, painters, poets we would have.*[20]

Larry Stone contributed to local consciousness of the arts and their potential impact on the community.

Traffic, transportation and congestion have become critical issues for Sunnyvale as they have for the entire region. Santa Clara County set about to decide whether the extension of the county light rail system should go to

Mountain View's downtown or Sunnyvale Town Center. Both options allowed for the light rail to travel by way of Lockheed Missiles and Space Company, which continued to be the largest employer in the county. In mid-1991, the County Transportation Subcommittee recommended that the extension go to Mountain View, even though both cities had lobbied long and hard for their own city. Bitter accusations from some Sunnyvale officials indicated a high level of frustration with the county for choosing the Mountain View alternative.

As Sunnyvale emerged as the "heart of Silicon Valley," new opportunities arose for the community to redefine itself. The concentration of electronics companies and the accolades for its municipal efficiency are new ingredients of an emerging, albeit impersonal identity. Other factors like Pacific Rim immigration, historical consciousness, political activism, and public display of art are all much more colorful aspects of the character of this city.

Chapter 9

REFLECTIONS ON SUNNYVALE'S HISTORY

Several recurring themes emerge from a careful study of the history of Sunnyvale. One theme is the degree to which the City of Sunnyvale is part of a larger picture, intricately involved with the county, the region, California and the federal government. While it is tempting to try to analyze Sunnyvale in isolation, outside factors have had major influence in forming Sunnyvale's identity. From the construction of the San Francisco-San José Railroad through the establishment of Moffett Field to World War II, federal defense contracts funding and the eventual possibility of base closure, Sunnyvale would be an entirely different place if it were not part of Silicon Valley and San Francisco Bay Area.

An understanding of how Sunnyvale fits into the bigger picture requires a sense of regional relationships. When Naval Air Station Sunnyvale was established in the 1930s, cooperation was the watchword of the day. However, twenty years later, in the 1950s, selfish isolationism ruled in Sunnyvale and Santa Clara County when Dutch Hamann's "panzer division" waged annexation wars. Regional cooperation continues to elude us as we battle over possible routes for rapid transit and future uses of military bases.

Another theme that runs through Sunnyvale's history is a sense that people believed change and development were "inevitable." Very few questioned "progress" or formulated alternatives and those that did were largely ignored. In the 1950s, Al Spiers told the farmers to sell their land because development was inevitable. Although much

beloved, the Murphy family home and old city hall were razed to make way for "progress" and a mammoth shopping mall was viewed as an "inevitable" solution to downtown's problems. Justifying change because it was "inevitable" alleviated personal and collective responsibility for social and political decisions. Could planning and cooperation have saved some farm land in Sunnyvale? Could funds have been scraped together to save the historic Murphy homestead? Could the Taaffe Street shopping center been converted to accommodate new merchants while maintaining the "heart" of Sunnyvale? A history such as this can point to moments of change and illuminate the decision-making process. My hope is that future choices reflect broader public participation and at the same time, accountability from government officials.

A third theme woven through the history is that attempts to cure one ill can lead to a whole new set of problems. The post-World War II development binge was to be the cure-all for unemployment. It worked. However, growth was not adequately monitored, resulting in suburban sprawl with a new generation of problems. Likewise, contracts from the defense department were thought to bolster a sagging industrial economy. For a time, the economy was supported by the contracts but they ultimately created dependence on the federal government, spawning new issues of contention. The panacea for this dependency was a shift to the design and production of high-tech consumer goods. Some problems resulting from the concentration of electronics companies in Silicon Valley are air and water pollution, traffic congestion, and housing shortages. The solutions generated to solve the problems throughout Sunnyvale's history have worked in the short-term, but more comprehensive, long-term answers always seem needed.

Sunnyvale has suffered from an identity crisis. As researcher Michael Otten concluded, residents of Sunnyvale "do not seem to have a strong sense of belonging."[1] The demolition of the Murphy house, city hall and old downtown has removed what had formerly been the visible "heart" of the town. New attempts at community involvement allow for a stronger identity to emerge from schools, parks, dramatic and fine arts, and recreational and cultural events. Programs like Leadership Sunnyvale, instituted in 1985, seek to broaden the perspective of their participants in public affairs, environmental issues, community services, and at the same time examine the character of the city and possible paths to future civic and social participation of its citizens. Sunnyvale's Patent Clearinghouse, arts programs and NOVA also contribute to molding an updated identity for the city.

The late novelist Wallace Stegner described a feeling of "placelessness" or being lost when he knew nothing about a particular place. "I know about the excitement of newness and possibility, but I also know the dissatisfaction and hunger that result from placelessness."[2] Although he was not referring specifically to Sunnyvale, his sentiment can certainly be applied all over Silicon Valley where thousands of residents have come from other parts of the nation or the world, and are completely unfamiliar with the history of this place. A city like Sunnyvale runs the risk of a lost identity unless it preserves some of its visible roots and written history.

The themes that are woven through the history of Sunnyvale provide a basis for reflection on community participation in decision-making for the city. Future choices need to have broad public participation. Citizens identifying themselves as part of an alive, vibrant town with a colorful past will be more likely to take an active role in making their city a good place to live and work ■

ABOUT THE AUTHOR

Mary Jo Ignoffo was born in Chicago, raised in Los Angeles, and has lived in Santa Clara County since 1974 when she entered Santa Clara University. Ignoffo holds a Bachelor's Degree from Santa Clara (1978) and a Master's Degree in history from San Jose State University (1991). Her primary interest is in local history. She has researched and authored historical articles and exhibits, including De Anza College's 25th Anniversary exhibit *De Anza Odyssey: The First Quarter Century*.

TABLES

Table 3

MAYORS OF SUNNYVALE

H. R. Fuller	1913-1914	James B. Scott	1962-1963
J. T. Brent	1915-1917	Eugene N. Conrardy	1965-1966
L. Larson	1918-1919	William F. Fernandez	1966-1967
P. R. Wightman	1920-1923	Donald E. Koreski	1967-1968
Edwina A. Benner	1924-1925		1975-1976
	1938-1939	Richard D. Hayden	1968-1969
F. E. Cornell	1926-1927	Harold C. Shields	1969-1970
Wm. McLaughlin	1928	Donald S. Logan	1970-1971
F. M. Drew	1929		1976-1977
George M. Wilhelmy	1930-1931	Charles H. Hefferlin	1971-1972
Anton Schmitz	1932-1933	Etta S. Albert	1972-1973
Albert L. Swanson	1934-1935	Gilbert R. Gunn	1973-1974
Frank R. White	1936		1978-1979
John E. Stowell	1937	Charley C. Allen	1974-1975
W. G. Fleckner	1940-1941	Lawrence E. Stone	1979-1980
Waldo R. Waelty	1942-1943		1987-1989
E. J. Corboline	1944-1945	Dianne McKenna	1980-1981
Otis B. Raines	1946-1947		1982-1983
Chris S. Webber	1948-1949	Ron Gonzales	1981-1982
Walter L. Jones	1949-1953		1986-1987
	1959-1960	Lynn Briody	1983-1984
	1964-1965	John E. Mercer	1984-1985
R. B. Gilmore	1953-1954	Brian O'Toole	1985-1986
Ernest N. Stout	1955-1957		1989-1990
Thomas M. Ryan	1957-1958	Richard Napier	1990-1991
Mark E. Russell	1960-1961	Patricia Castillo	1991-1993
Fred J. Logan	1961-1962	Frances Rowe	1993-
	1963-1964		

Source: Compiled by the City of Sunnyvale

Table 4

CITY MANAGERS OF SUNNYVALE

H. K. Hunter	1949-1958
Perry Scott	1958-1964
Thomas Sweeney	1964-1966
Gordon R. Miller (acting)	1966-1967
John E. Dever	1967-1977
Lee S. Ayers	1977-1979
Thomas F. Lewcock	1979-

Source: Compiled by the City of Sunnyvale

ENDNOTES

Chapter 1

BEFORE SUNNYVALE: THE LAND AND THE PEOPLE

[1] For a detailed discussion of early California ecology see: David W. Mayfield, "Ecology of the Pre-Spanish San Francisco Bay Area" (Ph.D. diss., San Francisco State University, 1978).

[2] R.E. Taylor and others, "Middle Holocene Age of the Sunnyvale Human Skeleton," Science, June 17, 1983: 273.

[3] Some helpful sources for information on early Bay Area inhabitants are Robert F. Heizer, ed., The Costanoan Indians, Local History Studies, vol. 18 (Cupertino, CA: California History Center, 1974); Malcolm Margolin, The Ohlone Way (Berkeley: Heyday Books, 1978); and Mayfield, "Ecology of the Pre-Spanish San Francisco Bay Area."

[4] Stanley Young, The Missions of California (San Francisco: Chronicle Books, 1988), 105.

[5] Walter Bean and James J. Rawls, California: An Interpretive History, 5th ed. (New York: McGraw-Hill Book Co., 1988), 18-19.

[6] Alfred Doten, The Journals of Alfred Doten 1849-1903, vol. 1, Walter Van Tilburg, ed. (Reno: University of Nevada Press, 1973), 410.

[7] Ibid., 328.

[8] Mildred Gentry Winters, "Mariano Castro," research paper, n.d., Castro Collection, Box 8, California History Center, Cupertino.

[9] Bertha M. Rice, The Women of Our Valley, Vol. 1 (San Jose, CA: Bertha M. Rice, 1955), 126.

[10] Johann A. Sutter, Diary of John Sutter (Palo Alto, CA: Grabhorn Press, 1932), 20.

[11] Bayard Taylor, El Dorado, vol. 1 (reprint of 1850 edition, Palo Alto, CA: Lewis Osborn, 1968), 230.

[12] United States, Bureau of the Census, unpublished manuscript, Fremont Township, Santa Clara County, California, 1880, p. 49.

[13] Sister Gabrielle Sullivan, Martin Murphy, Jr.: California Pioneer 1844-1884, Pacific Center for Western Historical Studies (Stockton, CA: University of Pacific, 1974), 16.

[14] George P. Hammond, ed., The Larkin Papers: Personal, Business, and Official Correspondence of Thomas Oliver Larkin, Merchant and United States Consul in California, Vol. V., 1846 (Berkeley: University of California Press, 1955), 119-120.

[15] Sullivan, Martin Murphy, Jr., 17.

[16] Elizabeth Carroll Whittier, "Pastoria de las Borregas Rancho: Home of Mr. and Mrs. Martin Murphy," in Helen Weber Kennedy and Veronica K. Kinzie, eds., Vignettes of the Gardens of San Jose de Guadalupe (San Francisco: San Francisco Garden Club, 1938), 37.

[17] Doten, The Journals of Alfred Doten, 324.

[18] Bean and Rawls, California, 122.

[19] Doten, The Journals of Alfred Doten, 428.

[20] United States Census, Santa Clara County, California, 1860, Roll #65, p. 216.

[21] Ibid., 1870, Roll #88, p. 50.

[22] Paul W. Gates, ed., California Ranchos and Farms 1846-1862 Including the Letters of John Quincy Adams Warren of 1861, Being Largely Devoted to Livestock, Wheat Farming, Fruit Raising, and the Wine Industry (Madison, WI: The State Historical Society of Wisconsin, 1967), 50.

[23] United States Census, Santa Clara County, California 1870, Roll #88, p. 50.

[24] All of the information on the anniversary party has been gleaned from newspaper accounts. They are San Jose Mercury, June 15, 1881; San Francisco Examiner, July 17 & 19, 1881; San Francisco Chronicle, July 19, 1881; San Jose Pioneer, July 23, 1881; San Jose Weekly Mercury, July 21, 1881.

[25] There is great discrepancy as to the number of guests. One source says as many as 50,000 guests arrived. See Patrick J. Dowling, California The Irish Dream (San Francisco: Golden Gate Publishers, 1989), 120.

[26] Sullivan, Martin Murphy, Jr., 14.

[27] Taylor, El Dorado, 231.

[28] Timothy Lukes and Gary Y. Okihiro, Japanese Legacy (Cupertino, CA: California History Center, De Anza College, 1985), 3, 11.

[29] Gates, California Ranchos, 50.

[30] Sullivan, Martin Murphy, Jr., 58.

[31] Yvonne Jacobson, Passing Farms, Enduring Values: California's Santa Clara Valley (Los Altos: William Kaufmann, Inc., 1984), 66.

[32] Sullivan, Martin Murphy, Jr., 68.

[33] Kent L. Seavey, Images: Sunnyvale's Heritage Resources (Sunnyvale: City of Sunnyvale and the California History Center, 1988), 37-38.

[34] George Briggs, "Life in Santa Clara County in the Fifties," September 28, 1895, copy in the Ann Hines Collection, Sunnyvale.

[35] Lukes and Okihiro, Japanese Legacy, 15.

[36] Carey McWilliams, Factories in the Field: The Story of Migratory Farm Labor in California (Boston: Little, Brown and Company, 1939), 59-60.

[37] Marjorie Pierce, ". . . And the Valley Was Filled With Orchards," n.d., clipping in the Ann Hines Collection, Sunnyvale.

[38] United States Census Manuscript, Santa Clara County, California, 1900 and 1910.

[39] Lukes and Okihiro, Japanese Legacy, 5.

[40] Ibid., 69.

[41] J. Donald Fisher, "A Historical Study of the Migrant in California" (Master's Thesis, University of Southern California, 1945; Reprinted San Francisco: R and E Associates, 1973), 9.

[42] Guinn, J., History of the State of California and Biographical Record of Coast Counties, California (Chicago: Chapman Publishing Company, 1904), 689.

[43] James T. Vargas and Joanne Smith, "The Portuguese: Manuel Vargas," in Sunnyvale City of Destiny, ed. California History Center, Local History Studies, vol. 17 (Cupertino, CA: De Anza College, 1974), 45.

[44] Letter from Harold Willson to Yvonne Jacobson, n.d., Michelle Jacobson Collection, California History Center, Cupertino.

Chapter 2

"CITY OF DESTINY"

[1] There has been debate whether Mr. Crossman's given name was William or Walter. I call him Walter based on the following sources: Santa Clara County Great Register (voter registration), 1890; 1920 Census Manuscript, Los Angeles County, California; his obituary in the Los Angeles Times, March 11, 1926; and Rockwell Hunt, ed. California and Californians, vol. III, (San Francisco: The Lewis Publishing Company, 1932) 101.

[2] Walter N. Frickstad, ed., A Century of California Post Offices, 1848-1954 (Oakland: Philatelic Research Society, 1955).

[3] Frank Bruno, "God's Country," in City of Destiny, 41.

[4] Collier's National Weekly, April 6, 1912, p. 40.

[5] "The Last Farm," Valley Journal, August 11, 1988.

[6] Sunnyvale Standard, November 27, 1914.

[7] See for example Santa Clara County Deeds, Book 334 page 495; and Book 215 page 594.

[8] San Jose Mercury, April 21, 1906.

[9] Ibid., April 22, 1906.

[10] George F. Gayer, "The Iron Men of Hendy," ed. Vernita Eubank and James Van de Erve, unpublished manuscript, Silicon Valley Library, Westinghouse Pamphlet file, 1985, 6.

[11] Ibid.

[12] Sunnyvale Standard, June 2, 1908

[13] Sunset Magazine, Development Section, February 1908.

[14] "Memories Still Clear," Sunnyvale Standard, February 1969.

[15] Sunnyvale Land Company, "Sunnyvale: 'The City of Destiny,'" Black Cat Press, 1908, copy in Pamphlet file, Sunnyvale Public Library.

[16] Sunset, February 1908.

[17] "75 Years, The Story of Your City and Sunnyvale Chamber of Commerce, 1906-1981," Supplement to Valley Journal, n.d., Pamphlet file, Sunnyvale Public Library.

[18] California History Center, City of Destiny, 21-22.

[19] "'City of Destiny' Votes to Become Incorporated," San Jose Mercury, December 11, 1912.

[20] Sunnyvale Standard, December 13, 1912

[21] San Francisco Chronicle, April 6, 1913, p. 39.

[22] Sunnyvale Sun, January 31, 1913.

[23] San Francisco Chronicle, May 27, 1911, p. 13.

[24] Sunnyvale Sun, September 3, 1915.

Chapter 3

A FARMING COMMUNITY

[1] "The Immigrants Santa Clara County Wants," Sunnyvale Standard, September 5, 1913.

[2] Sucheng Chan, This Bittersweet Soil: The Chinese in California Agriculture, 1860-1910 (Berkeley: University of California Pressm 1986), 420; and Bean and Rawls, California, 260-61.

[3] United States Census, Santa Clara County, Sunnyvale, California, 1920, e.d. 198, sheet 8.

[4] Mountain View Public Library, ed., Bittersweet: Memories of Old Mountain View, Vol. II: The Spanish, Oral History Project (Mountain View: Mountain View Public Library, 1980), 83-85.

[5] Judy Esteban, "The Spanish in Sunnyvale" (Research paper, California History Center, De Anza College, 1974), 3.

[6] Gayer, "Iron Men of Hendy," 9.

[7] Sunnyvale Standard, 1917, copy of clipping in possession of the author.

[8] Jacobson, Passing Farms, 165.

[9] Sunnyvale Standard, August 24, 1917.

[10] Ibid., December 7, 1917.

[11] Ibid., July 11, 1919.

[12] Nadine Tubbs, "Memories of the Old Post Office," in City of Destiny, 35.

[13] Rice, The Women of Our Valley, 63.

[14] Yvonne Jacobson, "Champion of Suffrage: Elizabeth Lowe Watson, 1843-1927," Californian, December 1993, p 11.

[15] Sophia Durst, Mosaics, (Berkeley: The Professional Press, 194?).

[16] Carole Pavlina, "The Yugoslavs: The Harvest of a 'Poor Man's Paradise'" in City of Destiny, 28.

[17] Edward Fassett, S.J., Interview with the author, February 9 & 19, 1991.

[18] San Jose Mercury News, May 11, 1991.

[19] United States Census, Population, Published Reports, California, Santa Clara County, 1930.

[20] Rudy Calles, "'Prune Heaven'" Pacific Historian (Spring 1979): 64.

[21] Sunnyvale Standard, August 15, 1930.

[22] Glenna Matthews, "The Fruit Workers of the Santa Clara Valley: Alternative Paths to Union Organization During the 1930s," Pacific Historical Review 54 (February 1985): 55.

[23] California History Center, Elizabeth Nicholas: Libby's Cannery Workers' Project, produced by De Anza College, 45 min., De Anza College, 1984, videocassette.

[24] Matthews, "Fruit Workers," 53.

[25] California History Center, Elizabeth Nicholas.

[26] Matthews, "Fruit Workers," 58.

Chapter 4

MILITARY BUILDUP IN SUNNYVALE

[1] Gladys Williamson, "Lady on the Go Given Recognition," n.d., newspaper clipping, Pamphlet file, Alameda County Library/Fremont Main Library.

[2] Spencer Gleason, Naval Air Station Moffett Field California: Silver Anniversary 1933-1958 (San Francisco: Globe, 1958), 5.

[3] "Airbase Finance Plan Undertaken," n.d., Whipple Collection, California History Center, Cupertino.

[4] Sunnyvale Standard, June 20, 1930.

[5] Laura Whipple in a letter to Mabel Bogart, 1930, Whipple Collection, California History Center, Cupertino.

[6] "Lindy Urges Sunnyvale: Station to Cost 4 Million," n.d., Whipple Collection, California History Center, Cupertino.

[7] Gleason, Naval Air Station Moffett Field, 5.

[8] Times Tribune, ed., Moffett-1989 (Palo Alto: Times Tribune, 1989) 3.

[9] Ibid., 4.

[10] "Woman Who Started Drive to Create Moffett Field to be Honored Friday," Palo Alto Times, September 27, 1962, Whipple Collection, California History Center, Cupertino.

[11] Paul Gullixson, Home Port for Sky Cruisers 1931-1935 (Palo Alto, CA: University National Bank & Trust Company, 1992), 1.

[12] San Jose Mercury, February 19, 1932.

[13] Times Tribune, Moffett-1989, 3.

[14] J. Gordon Vaeth, "U.S.S. *Macon*: Lost and Found," National Geographic, vol. 181, no. 1 (January 1992): 114-127.

[15] Ibid., p. 118; and John Toland, The Great Dirigibles: Their Triumphs and Disasters (New York: Dover Publications, 1972), 288.

[16] Basil Clarke, The History of Airships (London: Herbert Jenkins, 1961), 155.

[17] Edwin P. Hartman, Adventures in Research: A History of Ames Research Center 1940-1965, NASA Center History Series (Washington, D.C.: National Aeronautics and Space Administration, 1970), 30.

[18] Pavlina, "The Yugoslavs," in City of Destiny, 29.

[19] Sunnyvale Standard, April 11, 1930, p. 4.

[20] Wayne Andrews, ed., Architecture, Ambitions, and Americans: A Social History of American Architecture, (New York: The Free Press, a division of MacMillan Publishing Co., 1978), 280.

[21] Gayer, "Iron Men of Hendy," 13.

[22] Ibid., 13-18.

[23] Sunnyvale Standard, January 9, 1942.

[24] Masayo Umezawa Duus, Unlikely Liberators: The Men of the 100th and 442nd, trans. by Peter Duus (Honolulu: University of Hawaii Press, 1987), 148.

[25] Sunnyvale Standard, March 27, 1942.

[26] Alan Goedsted, "The Iron Men of Hendy," in City of Destiny, 61.

[27] David Lewis, "The Gun That Never Killed Anyone," Valley Journal, December 14, 1989.

[28] Mountain View Public Library, Bittersweet, vol. III, p. 198.

[29] Ernesto Galarza, Merchants of Labor: The Mexican Bracero Story (Santa Barbara: McNally & Loftin, Publishers, 1964), 9-11.

[30] Luis Valdez, "Envisioning California," California History (Winter 1989/90): 162.

[31] Gerald Nash, The American West Transformed: The Impact of the Second World War (Bloomington, IN: Indiana University Press, 1985), 17.

[32] Ibid., 35.

Chapter 5

FAREWELL TO FARMS

[1] Al Spiers in California History Center, City of Destiny, 86; and "Spiers Helped Convert Sunnyvale into Industrial City," San Jose Mercury News, March 24, 1978, Sunnyvale Public Library, Pamphlet file.

[2] Harry Gunetti to Al Spiers, February 25, 1947, in City of Destiny, 91.

[3] Nash, <u>American West Transformed</u>, 11.

[4] <u>Sunnyvale Standard</u>, January 11, 1949, p. 1.

[5] Ibid., January 14, 1949, p. 1.

[6] Some articles that provide statistics and describe the process of combining departments include City of Sunnyvale, "Decade of Public Safety Sunnyvale, California," 1961, 1; H. K. Hunter, "An Integrated Public Safety Department," <u>Public Management</u> (May 1951): 107; and Hunter as quoted in Harry W. More, Jr., <u>The New Era of Public Safety</u> (Springfield, Il: Charles C. Thomas, Publisher, 1970), 66-68.

[7] Hunter, "Integrated Department," 105.

[8] Sarah Gregory and Andy Otewalt, "Billy Wetterstrom's Story: Rolling Along With the Tide" and Elaine Winslow and Joyce Kanke, "Emile Corboline's Story: Community Service, A Family Deal," 19, in Community-Experimental Based Alternative School, <u>Prune Pits: The Collective Stories of Early Sunnyvale-Cupertino Residents</u> (Sunnyvale, CA: The Alternative School, 1979), Sunnyvale Public Library.

[9] "'Don't Keep It' Say Sunnyvale Citizens About S.P. Depot," <u>Sunnyvale Standard</u>, January 13, 1951.

[10] Philip J. Trounstine and Terry Christensen, <u>Movers and Shakers: The Study of Community Power</u> (New York: St. Martin's Press, 1982), 93.

[11] Carl Heintze, "A.P. Hamann and San Jose's Manifest Destiny," California Pioneers Papers, California Room, Martin Luther King, Jr. Library, San Jose, n.d., 7.

[12] <u>San Francisco Chronicle</u>, February 18, 1954, p. 6.

[13] <u>Sunnyvale Standard</u>, January 9, 1957, p. 1.

[14] Ibid., January 8, 1957.

[15] Karl Belser, "The Making of Slurban America," <u>Cry California</u> 5 (Fall 1970): 6.

[16] Mary Miholovich, conversation with the author, February 8, 1991; and "A Custom Home Area in Sunnyvale," <u>San Francisco Chronicle</u>, August 15, 1954, p. 4(L).

[17] Ann Hines, "Building the Post-War Housing Dream... Joe Eichler, Influences & Innovations," research paper, May 1978, Ann Hines Collection, Sunnyvale.

[18] Harriet Willson, comments at Sunnyvale Historical Society Annual Dinner, April 1992 and conversation with the author August 13, 1992.

[19] Belser, "Slurban America," 18.

[20] "Sunnyvale Marks Another Chapter in Its Big Story," <u>San Francisco Chronicle</u>, June 8, 1960. p. 2.

[21] Al Spiers, "An Invitation to America's Industry," in <u>City of Destiny</u>, 88.

[22] William G. Phelps, <u>Wall Street Journal</u>, April 24, 1956.

[23] <u>San Francisco Chronicle</u>, November 4, 1953. p. 19.

[24] Alan Bernstein and others, <u>Silicon Valley: Paradise or Paradox? The Impact of High Technology Industry on Santa Clara County</u> (Mountain View, CA: Pacific Studies Center, 1977), 7.

[25] Annalee Saxenian, "The Genesis of Silicon Valley," in <u>Silicon Landscapes</u>, ed. Peter Hall and Ann Markusen (Boston: Allen & Unwin, 1985), 24-28.

[26] Greg Gianelli, "The Sunnyvale Man Who Brought Lockheed to Town," <u>Valley Journal</u>, May 31, 1990, p. 16; Robin Reynolds, "Watching Silicon Valley's Boom," <u>Valley Journal</u>, July 23, 1987, p. 1; and Mack Lundstrom, "Lockheed's Herschel Brown dies at 88," <u>San Jose Mercury News</u>, October 2, 1993, p. 1(B).

[27] Hartman, <u>Adventures in Research</u>, 307.

[28] Jack Foisie, "Sunnyvale to Get Big GM Plant," <u>San Francisco Chronicle</u>, March 31, 1956, p. 1.

[29] Sunnyvale Chamber of Commerce, "Sunnyvale, U.S.A.: The City With the Built-in Future," Sunnyvale Public Library, Pamphlet file.

[30] Jacobson, <u>Passing Farms</u>, 234.

[31] Sunnyvale Chamber of Commerce, Application for All-American City Award, 1958, Sunnyvale Public Library, Pamphlet file.

[32] "Sunnyvale Buys 250 Acre Mountain Park," <u>San Francisco Chronicle</u>, March 5, 1958, p. 8; and James Benet, "Some Space That's Not Vanishing," Ibid., March 9, 1958, p. 14.

Chapter 6

Sunnyvale's Schizophrenia

[1] "Rezoning Battle Brewing," Sunnyvale Daily Standard, June 18, 1963, p. 3.

[2] Ibid., February 11, 1964, p. 1.

[3] "Pavlina Turns To Syndicates, Offices and Apartment Units," Sunnyvale Standard, January 28, 1970.

[4] Jacobson, Passing Farms, 234.

[5] "A Decade of Progress," Sunnyvale Standard, January 28, 1970.

[6] R. L. Polk, Polk's City Directory, Sunnyvale 1966 (Monterey Park, CA: R. L. Polk & Co. Publishers, 1966), viii.

[7] "Furor Over Rezoning in Sunnyvale," San Francisco Chronicle, May 27, 1964, p. 32.

[8] A series of articles trace this conflict. They include almost daily entries from Sunnyvale Standard Register Leader December 16, 1966 through February 24, 1967.

[9] Dwight D. Eisenhower, "Farewell Address," January 1961.

[10] Charles Wollenberg, Golden Gate Metropolis: Perspectives on Bay Area History, Institute of Governmental Studies (Berkeley: University of California, Berkeley, 1985), 312.

[11] Ann Roell Markusen and Robin Block, "Defensive Cities: Military Spending, High Technology, and Human Settlements," in High Technology, Space, and Society, ed. Manuel Castells, Urban Affairs Annual Review, vol. 28 (Beverly Hills: Sage Publications, 1985), 107.

[12] Bank of America 1969 report "Focus on Santa Clara County," quoted by Peter Carey in Carolyn Caddes and Barbara Newton, Portraits of Success: Impressions of Silicon Valley Pioneers (Palo Alto, CA: Tioga Publishing, 1986), 2.

[13] Peter Barnes, "Sunnyvale: Prunes to Missiles," Newsweek, June 9, 1969, 77.

[14] Ibid.

[15] Ibid.

[16] "Star to Jones," Standard Register Leader, January 31, 1967.

[17] "Prudential Buys Industrial Park," San Jose Mercury News, February 8, 1972, p. 52.

[18] Jack Melchor, quoted in Caddes and Newton, Portraits of Success, 2.

[19] Sunnyvale Daily Standard, March 25, 1964.

[20] Sunnyvale Standard, October 9, 1969.

Chapter 7

"Heart Transplant"

[1] Don C. Hoefler, "Silicon Valley—U.S.A.," Electronic News, January 11,18, & 25, 1971.

[2] Bill Workman, "Fledgling Capitalists In Garages," San Francisco Chronicle, May 23, 1977, p. 4.

[3] Moira Johnston, "High Tech, High Risk, and High Life in Silicon Valley," National Geographic (October 1982): 468.

[4] John Dever as quoted in Ed Hering, "Sunnyvale's New Spurt of Growth," San Jose Mercury News, February 10, 1973.

[5] Sunnyvale Scribe, April 16, 1975.

[6] Ibid.

[7] William Moore, "The Vanishing Strawberry Fields," San Francisco Chronicle, July 21, 1976, 4.

[8] Pavlina, "The Yugoslavs," in City of Destiny, 31.

[9] Dever as quoted in Hering, "Spurt," San Jose Mercury News, February 10, 1973.

[10] Ed Hering, "Industrial Growth Debated," Ibid., March 17, 1973.

[11] Ibid., March 9, 1973.

[12] Valley Journal, November 17, 1973.

[13] Ibid.

[14] Jim Barrett, "Re-election is Secure but Unopposed Logan Isn't Ignoring Voters," Sunnyvale Scribe, March 12, 1975.

[15] Michael Otten as quoted in Jay Johnson, "Residents Lack Sense of Belonging," Valley Journal, January 29, 1975.

[16] You-Wen Hsieh, "The Redevelopment of Downtown Sunnyvale, California," (Master's Thesis, San Jose State University, 1979), 57.

[17] Sally Racanelli, "City Moves Forward on Redevelopment Plan for Downtown," The Sunnyvale American, June 24, 1976.

[18] Ibid.

[19] Larry Stone, Interview with the author, October 30, 1992.

[20] Sue Beving, "Heart Transplant for Sunnyvale," Peninsula Magazine, June 1978, p. 18.

[21] Ibid.

[22] Karen Goldman, "Fern Ohrt's Story: Saving the Trees," Pamphlet file, Sunnyvale Public Library, 1979.

[23] Fern Ohrt as quoted by S. L. Wykes, "Sunnyvale at 75: Model of Efficiency Seeks a Personality," San Jose Mercury News, May 9, 1987.

[24] "Businessman Battling City Hall Ouster Edict," Valley Journal, July 8, 1977.

[25] Beving, "Heart Transplant," Peninsula Magazine, June 1978, 20.

[26] Richard Hanner, "Angry Citizens," Valley Journal, May 24, 1978.

[27] Yvonne Jacobson, Passing Farms, 26.

Chapter 8

THE HEART OF SILICON VALLEY

[1] "How Sunnyvale and Cupertino Fared During the 1970s," Valley Journal, January 2, 1980.

[2] "Faces of the Future," San Jose Mercury News, September 17, 1989, 16A.

[3] Ibid.

[4] Andrew S. Grove, "The Future of Silicon Valley," California Management Review, 29 (Spring 1987): 158.

[5] AnnaLee Saxenian, "Silicon Chips and Spatial Structure: The Industrial Basis of Urbanization in Santa Clara County," (Master's Thesis, University of California, Berkeley, 1980), 2.

[6] City of Sunnyvale, "Socio-Economic Element of the General Plan," 1989.

[7] Barbara Buell, "Sunnyvale City Council OKs Industrial Growth Moratorium," Valley Journal, January 16, 1980, p. 1.

[8] Mark Nelson, "Chamber President Opposes No-growth Policy," Ibid., January 9, 1980, p. 1.

[9] Ann Hines, interview with the author, April 13, 1992.

[10] "The Centennial Celebration of California's Grandest Party," Advertising insert of Peninsula Times Tribune, July 17-19, 1981, copy in possession of the author.

[11] Kay Peterson, interview with the author, June 24, 1992.

[12] Lincoln Property Company, press release, 1987, copy in Sunnyvale Public Library, pamphlet file "Canneries."

[13] Andrews, Architecture, Ambitions, and Americans, 280.

[14] Sally Woodbridge, ed., Guide to Architecture in San Francisco and Northern California (San Francisco: Peregrine Press, 1973), 173.

[15] San Antonio Business Magazine, "Can a City Be Run Like a Business?", December 1986, 22.

[16] Bert Robinson, "Smitten With Sunnyvale," San Jose Mercury News, May 27, 1991, p. 1A.

[17] David Osborne and Ted Gaebler, Reinventing Government: How the Entrepreneurial Spirit is Transforming the Public Sector (Reading, MA: Addison Wesley Publishing Company, 1992).

[18] Bob Brownstein as quoted in Nick Anderson, "Sunnyvale is Efficient From Top to Bottom Line," San Jose Mercury News, September 10, 1993, p. 21 A.

[19] Thomas F. Lewcock and O. Jess Barba, "Managers and Police Chiefs: Friends or Foes?'" Public Management (June 1988): 4.

[20] Larry Stone, Speech at ICC Dinner Meeting, December 15, 1988.

Chapter 9

REFLECTIONS ON SUNNYVALE'S HISTORY

[1] Otten as quoted in Johnson, "Residents Lack Sense of Belonging," Valley Journal, January 29, 1975.

[2] Wallace Stegner, "A Sense of Place," San Jose Mercury News, April 26, 1992

ABOUT THE SOURCES

This account of Sunnyvale's history is based on a wide range of primary and secondary sources. The primary sources include newspaper accounts, especially from the <u>Sunnyvale Standard</u> which began publication in 1908. The <u>Valley Journal</u>, <u>San Jose Mercury News</u>, and <u>San Francisco Chronicle</u> were also important, particularly for events of the last twenty years. Wherever possible, page numbers accompany citations. However, some articles were found in clipping files and page numbers were not available.

City documents such as the city charter and general plan as well as chamber of commerce literature were useful to trace Sunnyvale's transition from a farming community to a modern city. County records such as property deeds, tax rolls and plat maps helped link individuals to specific properties. Federal census manuscripts offered insight into the ethnic makeup of Sunnyvale throughout its history.

Many archival collections contain sources about specific families or topics. Those housed at the California History Center are: the Castro Collection, the Whipple Collection, and the Michelle Ann Jacobson Collection. The Ann Hines Collection, in possession of Ann Hines, contains various clippings on Sunnyvale's history and specifically documents the historic preservation movement in Sunnyvale. The Sunnyvale Collection located at the Sunnyvale Public Library is a vast array of public documents, published and unpublished sources, microfilm, and pamphlet files. It also has a collection of scrapbooks from the 1970s and 1980s which traces the ORCHARDS political movement.

Many photograph collections also served to make the town history a more personal one. The Sunnyvale Historical Society & Museum Association's collection includes 19th and 20th century photographs depicting town, family, civic, political, and religious events and specifically highlights the town's agricultural past. The Stocklmeir Library at the California History Center also maintains a photo archive and has many relating to Sunnyvale, especially the Michelle Ann Jacobson collection photos. Current and former residents also shared their photos.

Secondary sources include numerous county histories and several works on the fruit industry, war production, postwar development and Silicon Valley. Of particular interest were those works specifically relating portions of Sunnyvale's history such as Yvonne Jacobson's <u>Passing Farms: Enduring Values</u> (1984), the California History Center's <u>Sunnyvale: City of Destiny</u> (1974), <u>Images: Sunnyvale's Heritage Resources</u> by Kent Seavey (1988), and Sister Gabrielle Sullivan's <u>Martin Murphy, Jr.: California Pioneer 1844-1884</u> (1974).

In combination with the sources that follow, these helped to tell the story that is Sunnyvale's.

Selected Bibliography

Books:

Andrews, Wayne, ed. Architecture, Ambitions, and Americans: A Social History of American Architecture. New York: The Free Press, a division of MacMillan Publishing Company, 1978.

Bean, Walter and James J. Rawls. California: An Interpretive History. 5th ed. New York: McGraw-Hill Book Co., 1988.

Bernstein, Alan and Bob DeGrasse, Rachael Grossman, Chris Paine, and Lenny Siegel. Silicon Valley: Paradise or Paradox? The Impact of High Technology Industry on Santa Clara County. Mountain View, CA: Pacific Studies Center, 1977.

Caddes, Carolyn and Barbara Newton. Portraits of Success: Impressions of Silicon Valley Pioneers. Palo Alto, CA: Tioga Publishing, 1986.

California History Center, ed. Sunnyvale, City of Destiny. Cupertino, CA: California History Center, De Anza College, 1974.

Chan, Sucheng. This Bittersweet Soil: The Chinese in California Agriculture, 1860-1910. Berkeley: University of California Press, 1986.

Clark, Basil. The History of Airships. London: Herbert Jenkins, 1961.

Community-Experimental Based Alternative School. Prune Pits: The Collective Stories of Early Sunnyvale-Cupertino Residents. Sunnyvale: The Alternative School, 1979.

Doten, Alfred. The Journals of Alfred Doten, Vol. 1-3. Walter Van Tilburg Clark, ed. Reno: University of Nevada Press, 1973.

Dowling, Patrick J. California The Irish Dream. San Francisco: Golden Gate Publishers, 1989.

Durst, Sophia. Mosaics. Berkeley: The Professional Press, 194?.

Duus, Masayo Umezawa. Unlikely Liberators: The Men of the 100th and 442nd. Translated by Peter Duus. Honolulu: University of Hawaii Press, 1987.

Frickstad, Walter N., ed. A Century of California Post Offices, 1848-1954. Oakland: Philatelic Research Society, 1955.

Galarza, Ernesto. Merchants of Labor: The Mexican Bracero Story. Santa Barbara: McNally & Loftin, Publishers, 1964.

Gates, Paul W., ed. California Ranchos and Farms 1846-1862 Including the Letters of John Quincy Adams Warren of 1861, Being Largely Devoted to Livestock, Wheat Farming, Fruit Raising, and the Wine Industry. Madison, WI: The State Historical Society of Wisconsin, 1967.

Gleason, Spencer. Naval Air Station Moffett Field California: Silver Anniversary 1933-1958. San Francisco: Globe, 1958.

Guinn, J. History of the State of California and Biographical Record of Coast Counties, California. Chicago: Chapman Publishing Company, 1904.

Gullixson, Paul. Home Port for Sky Cruisers 1931-1935. Palo Alto: University National Bank & Trust Company, 1992.

Hammond, George P., ed. The Larkin Papers: Personal, Business, and Official Correspondence of Thomas Oliver Larkin, Merchant and United States Consul in California. Berkeley: University of California Press, 1955.

Hartman, Edwin P. Adventures in Research: A History of Ames Research Center 1940-1965. NASA Center History Series. Washington, D.C.: National Aeronautics and Space Administration, 1970.

Heizer, Robert F. The Costanoan Indians. Cupertino, CA: California History Center, De Anza College, 1974.

Hunt, Rockwell, ed. California and Californians, Vol. III. San Francisco: The Lewis Publishing Company, 1932.

Jacobson, Yvonne. Passing Farms, Enduring Values: California's Santa Clara Valley. Los Altos: William Kaufmann, Inc., 1984.

Kennedy, Helen W. and Veronica K. Kinzie, eds. Vignettes of the Gardens of San Jose de Guadalupe. San Francisco: San Francisco Garden Club, 1938.

Lukes, Timothy and Gary Y. Okihiro. Japanese Legacy. Cupertino, CA: California History Center, De Anza College, 1985.

Margolin, Malcolm. The Ohlone Way. Berkeley: Heyday Books, 1978.

McWilliams, Carey. Factories in the Field: The Story of Migratory Farm Labor in California. Boston: Little, Brown and Company, 1939.

More, Harry W. Jr. The New Era of Public Safety. Springfield, IL: Charles C. Thomas Publisher, 1970.

Mountain View Public Library, ed. <u>Bittersweet: Memories of Old Mountain View, Vol. II: The Spanish</u>. Oral History Project. Mountain View, CA: Mountain View Public Library, 1980.

Nash, Gerald D. <u>The American West Transformed: The Impact of the Second World War</u>. Bloomington, IN: Indiana University Press, 1985.

Osborne, David and Ted Gaebler. <u>Reinventing Government: How the Entrepreneurial Spirit is Transforming the Public Sector</u>. Reading, MA: Addison Wesley Publishing Company, 1992.

Polk, R. L. <u>Polk's City Directory</u>, Sunnyvale, 1966. Monterey Park, CA: R. L. Polk & Company Publishers, 1966.

Rice, Bertha M. <u>The Women of Our Valley</u>, vol. 1. San Jose, CA: Bertha M. Rice, 1955.

Seavey, Kent L. <u>Images: Sunnyvale's Heritage Resources</u>. Sunnyvale: City of Sunnyvale and California History Center, 1988.

Sullivan, Gabrielle. <u>Martin Murphy, Jr.: California Pioneer 1844-1884</u>. Pacific Center for Western Historical Studies. Stockton, CA: University of Pacific, 1974.

Sutter, Johann A. <u>Diary of John Sutter</u>. Palo Alto, CA: Grabhorn Press, 1932.

Taylor, Bayard. <u>El Dorado</u>, Vol.1. Palo Alto, CA: Lewis Osborn, 1968.

<u>Times Tribune</u>, ed. <u>Moffett-1989</u>. Palo Alto, CA: <u>Times Tribune</u>, 1989.

Toland, John. <u>The Great Dirigibles: Their Triumphs and Disasters</u>. New York: Dover Publications, 1972.

Trounstine, Philip J. and Terry Christensen. <u>Movers and Shakers: The Study of Community Power</u>. New York: St. Martin's Press, 1982.

Wollenberg, Charles. <u>Golden Gate Metropolis: Perspectives on Bay Area History</u>. Institute of Governmental Studies. Berkeley: University of California, Berkeley, 1985.

Woodbridge, Sally, ed. <u>Guide to Architecture in San Francisco and Northern California</u>. San Francisco: Peregrine Press, 1973.

Young, Stanley. <u>The Missions of California</u>. San Francisco: Chronicle Books, 1988.

ARTICLES:

Barnes, Peter. "Sunnyvale: Prunes to Missiles," <u>Newsweek</u>, June 9, 1969, 77.

Belser, Karl. "The Making of Slurban America." <u>Cry California</u> 5 (Fall 1970): 1-18.

Beving, Sue. "Heart Transplant for Sunnyvale." <u>Peninsula Magazine</u>, June 1978, 18-20, & 36.

Calles, Rudy. "'Prune Heaven.'" <u>Pacific Historian</u> 23 (Spring 1979): 58-61.

Grove, Andrew S. "The Future of Silicon Valley." <u>California Management Review</u>, 29 (Spring 1987): 154-58.

Hoefler, Don C. "Silicon Valley—U.S.A." <u>Electronic News</u>, 11, 18, & 25 January 1971.

Hunter, H. K. "An Integrated Public Safety Department." <u>Public Management</u> (May 1951): 105-107.

Jacobson, Yvonne. "Champion of Suffrage: Elizabeth Lowe Watson, 1843-1927." <u>The Californian</u> (December 1993): 6-11.

Johnston, Moira. "High Tech, High Risk, and High Life in Silicon Valley." <u>National Geographic</u>, October 1982, 459-77.

Lewcock, Thomas F. and O. Jess Barba. "Managers and Police Chiefs: Friends or Foes?" <u>Public Management</u> June 1988: 2-4.

Markusen, Ann Roell and Robin Block. "Defensive Cities: Military Spending, High Technology, and Human Settlements." In <u>High Technology, Space, and Society</u>, ed. Manuel Castells. Urban Affairs Annual Reviews, vol. 28. Beverly Hills: Sage Publications, 1985, 106-113.

Matthews, Glenna. "The Fruit Workers of the Santa Clara Valley: Alternative Paths to Union Organization During the 1930s." <u>Pacific Historical Review</u> 54 (February 1985): 51-70.

<u>San Antonio Business Magazine</u>. "Can a City Be Run Like a Business?" <u>San Antonio Business Magazine</u>, December 1986, 22-29.

Saxenian, AnnaLee. "The Genesis of Silicon Valley." In <u>Silicon Landscapes</u>, ed. Peter Hall and Ann Markusen. Boston: Allen & Unwin, 1985: 20-34.

Sunset Magazine, Development Section, February 1908.

Taylor, R. E., Louis A. Payen, Bert Gerow, D. J. Donahue, T.H. Zabel, A. J. T. Jull, P. E. Damon. "Middle Holocene Age of the Sunnyvale Human Skeleton." Science (June 17,1983): 271-73.

Vaeth, J. Gordon. "USS Macon: Lost and Found." National Geographic, January 1992, 114-127.

Valdez, Luis. "Envisioning California." California History (Winter 1989/90): 162-65.

THESES OR RESEARCH PAPERS:

Esteban, Judy. "The Spanish in Sunnyvale." Research paper, California History Center, De Anza College, 1974.

Fisher, J. Donald. "A Historical Study of the Migrant in California." Master's thesis, University of Southern California, 1945; Reprinted San Francisco: R and E Associates, 1973.

Goldman, Karen. "Fern Ohrt's Story: Saving the Trees." Pamphlet file, Sunnyvale Public Library, 1979.

Heintze, Carl. "A.P. Hamann and San Jose's Manifest Destiny." California Pioneer Papers, California Room, Martin Luther King, Jr. Library, San Jose, n.d.

Hines Ann. "Building the Post-war Housing Dream . . . Joe Eichler, Influences & Innovations." Ann Hines Collection, Sunnyvale, 1978.

Hsieh, You-Wen. "The Redevelopment of Downtown Sunnyvale, California." Master's thesis, San Jose State University, 1979.

Mayfield, David W. "Ecology of the Pre-Spanish San Francisco Bay Area." Ph.D. diss., San Francisco State University, 1978.

Saxenian, AnnaLee. "Silicon Chips and Spatial Structure: The Industrial Basis of Urbanization in Santa Clara County." Master's thesis, University of California, Berkeley, 1980.

Winters, Mildred G. "Mariano Castro." Castro Collection, Box 8, California History Center, De Anza College, Cupertino.

UNPUBLISHED MANUSCRIPT:

Gayer, George F. "The Iron Men of Hendy." Edited by Vernita Eubank and James Van de Erve. Silicon Valley Library, Westinghouse Pamphlet file #1, 1985.

NEWSPAPERS:

Collier's National Weekly, April 6, 1912, p.40.

Los Angeles Times, March 11, 1926.

Palo Alto Times, September 27, 1962.

Peninsula Times Tribune, July 17-19, 1981.

San Francisco Chronicle, July 19, 1881 and 1912-1990.

San Francisco Examiner, July 17 & 19, 1881.

San Francisco Morning Call, August 30, 1892.

San Jose Mercury News, 1881-1990.

San Jose Pioneer, July 23, 1881.

Sunnyvale American, June 24, 1976.

Sunnyvale Scribe, March- April, 1975.

Sunnyvale Standard, 1908-1980.

Sunnyvale Standard Register Leader, December 1966-April 1967.

Sunnyvale Sun, January 31, 1913.

Valley Journal, 1970-1990.

Wall Street Journal, April 24, 1956.

INTERVIEWS:

Fassett, S.J. Edward. Interview with the author. February 9 & 19, 1991.

Hines, Ann. Interview with the author. April 13 & 29, 1992.

Miller, Dorothy Raines. Interview with the author. September 20, 1991.

Miholovich, Mary. Conversation with the author. February 8, 1991.

Peterson, Kay. Interview with the author. June 24, 1992.

Ryan, Caroline. Interview with the author. November 23, 1992.

Stone, Larry. Interview with the author. October 30, 1992.

Willson, Harriet. Interview with the author. August 13, 1992.

OTHER SOURCES:

City of Sunnyvale. "Decade of Public Safety Sunnyvale, California,"
        1961.

City of Sunnyvale. "Socio-Economic Element of the General
        Plan,"1989.

Santa Clara County Great Register, 1890.

Sunnyvale Chamber of Commerce. Application for All-American City
        Award, 1958. Pamphlet file Sunnyvale Public Library.

Sunnyvale Chamber of Commerce. "Sunnyvale, U.S.A.: The City With
        the Built-in Future," 1956. Pamphlet file Sunnyvale Public
        Library.

United States. Bureau of the Census. Unpublished manuscripts. Santa
        Clara County, California, 1860-1920.

United States. Bureau of the Census. Population. Published reports.
        California, Santa Clara County, 1920-1980.

VIDEORECORDINGS:

California History Center. Elizabeth Nicholas: Libby's Cannery
        Workers' Project. Produced by De Anza College. 45 min.
        California History Center, De Anza College, 1984. Videocas-
        sette.

Leadership Sunnyvale and Ann Hines. Collection of videos, 1991 and
        1992.

INDEX

Page entries in bold face refer to illustrations.